T0358179

Finance: A Characteristics Approach

Since the mid-1980s, the characteristics model in economics has been applied extensively to the field of finance, and offers a fresh perspective for understanding financial behaviour. It has enabled both the analyst and the investor to explore the characteristics of financial products, such as expected return, risk and marketability, as a dimension distinct from the substance of the product itself.

The first part of the volume explores the theoretical implications of such an approach. It examines:

- the characteristics model of portfolio behaviour and asset pricing
- the characteristics model as a unifying framework for analysing financial markets, financial intermediation and the process of financial innovation.

The remainder of the volume focuses on empirical applications of the characteristics model, including:

- computation of interest equivalence for nonprice characteristics of bank products
- analysis of financial innovations in short-term retail financial products.

The book therefore represents an invaluable asset for both the specialist financial economist, and the generalist economist seeking original source material.

David Blake is Professor of Financial Economics at Birkbeck College, University of London, and has worked at the London School of Economics, the London Business School and City University Business School. His previous publications include *Modelling Pension Fund Investment Behaviour, Pension Schemes and Pension Funds in the United Kingdom, A Short Course of Economics* and *Financial Market Analysis*.

Routledge International Studies in Money and Banking

1 Private Banking in Europe
Lynn Bicker

2 Bank Deregulation and Monetary Order
George Selgin

3 Money in Islam
A study in Islamic political economy
Masudul Alam Choudhury

4 The Future of European Financial Centres
Kirsten Bindemann

5 Payment Systems in Global Perspective
Maxwell J. Fry, Isaak Kilato, Sandra Roger, Krzysztof Senderowicz,
David Sheppard, Francisco Solis and John Trundle

6 What is Money?
John Smithin

7 Finance
A Characteristics Approach
Edited by David Blake

8 Organisational Change and Retail Finance
An Ethnographic Perspective
Richard Harper, Dave Randall and Mark Rouncefield

9 The History of the Bundesbank
Lessons for the European Central Bank
Jakob de Haan

10 The Euro
A Challenge and Opportunity for Financial Markets
Published on behalf of Société Universitaire Européenne de
Recherches Financières (SUERF)
Edited by Michael Artis, Axel Weber and Elizabeth Hennessy

Finance

A Characteristics Approach

Edited by David Blake

Routledge
Taylor & Francis Group

LONDON AND NEW YORK

First published 2000 by Routledge

Published 2019 by Routledge
2 Park Square, Milton Park, Abingdon, Oxon OX14 4RN
52 Vanderbilt Avenue, New York, NY.10017

Routledge is an imprint of the Taylor & Francis Group, an informa business

British Library Cataloguing in Publication Data
A catalogue record for this book is available from the British Library

Library of Congress Cataloging in Publication Data
Finance: a characteristics approach / [edited by] David Blake.
    p. cm.
  Includes bibliographical references and index.
  1. Finance—Mathematical models. I. Blake, David, 1954–
HG106.F56 2000
332 21–dc21   99-045910

ISBN 13: 978-0-415-21290-8 (hbk)

To Taylor and Lauren

Contents

List of figures x
List of tables xi
List of contributors xii

1 **Introduction** 1
DAVID BLAKE

   References 9

2 **Portfolio behaviour and asset pricing in a characteristics framework** 12
DAVID BLAKE

   2.1 Introduction 12
   2.2 The characteristics model of portfolio behaviour and asset pricing 13
   2.3 The characteristics model as a unifying framework for analysing portfolio behaviour and asset pricing 20
   2.4 Conclusion 32
   References 32

3 **Financial intermediation and financial innovation in a characteristics framework** 35
DAVID BLAKE

   3.1 Introduction 36
   3.2 The characteristics model of financial intermediation 37

3.3   The characteristics model of financial
      innovation 44
3.4   Conclusion 52
      References 53

4   A characteristics definition of financial markets   56
SHELAGH A. HEFFERNAN

4.1   Introduction 56
4.2   Financial products and financial markets:
      definitions 57
4.3   Regulatory and technological changes:
      the demand side 63
4.4   Regulatory and technological changes: the
      supply side 78
4.5   Conclusion 79
      Appendix 1 79
      Appendix 2 79
      References 81

**5   The computation of interest equivalences for the
     nonprice characteristics of bank products**   83
SHELAGH A. HEFFERNAN

5.1   Introduction 83
5.2   Methodology 85
5.3   Constructing the data series 87
5.4   Results 90
5.5   Computation of interest equivalences 92
5.6   Conclusion 94
      References 95

**6   A characteristics analysis of financial innovations in
     short-term retail financial products**   96
MEGHNAD DESAI AND WILLIAM LOW

6.1   Introduction 96
6.2   A characteristics framework 100
6.3   Data and measurement 103

6.4   An analytical view of innovation 117
6.5   Conclusion 126
    References 126

7   Postscript   127
DAVID BLAKE

Index   129

Figures

3.1 The effect of financial intermediation   42
4.1 Characteristics frontier for category A financial pro-
     ducts   59
4.2 Representing a particular point, N, on the efficiency
     plane   61
4.3 Higher r displaces point F vertically upwards   69
4.4 Higher q raises the plane $EGHJ$ 70
4.5 Lower spread shifts $EJKL$ towards origin on risk axis   71
4.6 dA_1 shifts efficiency plane from EFA to EFA_1 72
6.1 Two instruments: x_1 and x_2 101
6.2 A trivial innovation (x_3) and an important innova-
     tion (x_4)   103
6.3 The growth in financial assets available to house-
     holds   107
6.4 Financial assets available to households in April 1982   112
6.5 Financial assets available to households in May 1983   113
6.6 Financial assets available to households in May 1984   116
6.7 The change in θ over time   121
6.8 The change in the maximum θ over time   124
6.9 The limit to financial innovation   125

Tables

4.1 Classification of financial products in the character-
    istics model   62
4.2 The effects of parameter changes on B, D, M 68
4.3 The impact of regulatory changes on key parameters   72
4.4 Average touches (%) in the UK equity market   74
5.1 Interest equivalences for deposit products   93
5.2 Interest equivalences for loan products   94
6.1 Financial assets available to households in January
    1984   105
6.2 Number of assets over time (N_t)   106
6.3 Assets and their dates of introduction   108
6.4 Financial assets available to households in April 1982 110
6.5 Financial assets available to households in May 1983   114
6.6 Financial assets available to households in May 1984   118
6.7 Size distribution of $\hat{\theta}_i$ (January 1982 to December
    1984)   120
6.8 θ_t^*: the maximum gap   123

Contributors

David **Blake** is Professor of Financial Economics at Birkbeck College, University of London.

Lord **Meghnad Desai** is Professor at the Centre for the Study of Global Governance, London School of Economics, University of London.

Shelagh A. Heffernan is Professor at the Department of Banking and Finance, City University Business School, London.

William Low is at the University of Northern British Columbia.

Chapter 1

Introduction

David Blake

The origins of the characteristics model in economics date back to the mid-1950s. The earliest applications analysed the demand for related goods (such as various types of food) in terms of the common set of characteristics or attributes embodied in them (such as taste, nutritiousness, hunger relief, preparation time, etc.), rather than in terms of the specific items of food that individuals consumed (such as bread, haddock, eggs, beef and so on) (see especially Gorman, 1959, 1980; also Stone, 1956). Productive activity, in particular the relationship between a firm's outputs and its factors of production (such as labour, capital and land), was also analysed in terms of characteristics (see Makower, 1957). The principal objective of the characteristics framework is to simplify the analysis of complex relationships by modelling the behaviour of a large group of variables in terms of a much smaller set of measurable characteristics that are common to the larger group. For example, the preferences of consumers over a vast range of different food items can be given an equivalent but simplified representation in terms of a much smaller number of common characteristics, on the grounds that consumers are in reality interested in 'consuming' these characteristics rather than the particular items of food that deliver the characteristics.

The characteristics model was popularised in the 1960s and early 1970s by Lancaster (1966, 1971). The 1970s and early 1980s saw the publication of a series of empirical applications of the model, ranging from an analysis of the UK National Food Survey which covers more than 150 different foods purchased for consumption in the home (see Boyle *et al.*, 1977; Pudney, 1980, 1981a, b), through studies of quality measurement (see Lucas, 1975; Triplett, 1976; Klevmarken, 1977) and consumer durables (see Cragg and Uhler,

1970; Griliches, 1971), to analyses explaining the introduction of new commodities (see Ironmonger, 1972). Pudney, for example, found that the characteristics model is 'more flexible in its modelling of demand interactions than [other] systems, and ... is also capable of incorporating extraneous information on the physical relatedness of different goods in a very satisfactory way' (1980, p. 876). 'Perhaps', he concluded, 'it is the model we should all be using' (1981b, p. 576). The characteristics model was also applied during this period to fields related to economics, such as marketing (see Hansen, 1972; Woodside *et al.*, 1977). By around 1980, the characteristics framework was well established as an important modelling tool in economics and a number of related disciplines (see Deaton and Muellbauer, 1980).

However, there was one discipline related to economics where the characteristics model had not been applied by the beginning of the 1980s and that was finance, although there had been a few hints in the literature about its potential usefulness to finance (see Tobin, 1958; Kane, 1972; Roberts, 1975; Sharpe, 1985). It was this lacuna that prompted a new programme of research in the late 1980s and early 1990s which culminated in the characteristics model being applied to a number of different areas of finance. The catalyst for this new programme was Blake's (1986) doctoral thesis at the London School of Economics, an institution where much of the research (both theoretical and empirical) on the characteristics model was initiated (see Gorman, 1972, 1976; Boyle *et al.*, 1977; Pudney, 1980, 1981a, b). This book brings together in a single source some of the key finance applications of the characteristics model.

The principal attraction of applying the characteristics model to finance is that investors are so obviously more interested in the characteristics of the financial products that they purchase than the products themselves. An investor buys a share in a company, not because of the particular security, nor even because of the particular company, but rather because of the attributes offered by that security in terms of, say, expected return, risk and marketability. Similarly, a depositor places money in a bank account, not because of the bank *per se*, but rather because of the properties of the account in terms of offering interest, liquidity, security, convenience of location, etc. Another example might be a financial innovation whereby a new asset is introduced because it has a more desirable combination of characteristics than existing assets. In this way, it is possible to see how the demand by investors for a large number of assets can be expressed in terms of the demand for a much smaller number of characteristics shared by those assets. The weakness of the model lies in any difficulty in measuring the characteristics of interest: how, for example, should an investigator measure expected return, risk or liquidity, and do these measures correspond sufficiently closely to those actually used by investors when constructing their portfolios of assets? However, this is a problem common to most economic modelling and is not unique to the characteristics model.

Chapter 2 (originally published as Blake, 1990) is a theoretical chapter which derives the characteristics model of portfolio behaviour and asset pricing. Portfolio behaviour concerns the efficient structuring of asset portfolios by individual investors. We show that the demand to hold assets in portfolios is a derived demand to hold the characteristics embodied in those assets. Assets are not held for their own sake, but for the configuration of characteristics they contain. Assets can be thought of as 'producing' characteristics and some combination of assets produces these characteristics more efficiently (i.e. at lower cost) than other combinations. The first step is to derive the efficient asset-characteristics technology, i.e. the production possibility (or efficiency) frontier between assets and characteristics: asset portfolios with the most efficient combinations of characteristics will lie on this frontier. In an efficient financial system, the task of establishing the efficiency frontier will be performed by the market itself rather than by individual investors. The second step is to derive the optimal demand for characteristics and the optimal derived demand for assets; investors can be thought of as 'consuming' the characteristics embodied in these assets. These demands will differ between investors, since different investors will prefer different combinations of characteristics. For example, some investors will have a stronger preference for liquidity and a greater aversion to risk than other investors, and such investors will choose asset combinations with higher exposure to the desirable characteristic (liquidity) and a lower exposure to the undesirable characteristic (risk) than these other investors. The demand functions for assets will depend on asset prices, the technological relationship between assets and characteristics, and the preferences for characteristics.

Once we have derived individual investors' demands for assets, we can aggregate over these demands to generate the market demands for assets. By taking into consideration market supplies of assets, we can solve for equilibrium prices and hence generate the characteristics model of asset prices. The chapter ends by showing that the characteristics model provides a unifying framework for analysing many existing preference-based models of portfolio behaviour and asset pricing, e.g. the state-preference model, the parameter-preference model, the capital asset pricing model, the intertemporal capital asset pricing model and the ARCH-in-mean pricing model.

Chapter 3 (originally published as Blake, 1996) demonstrates that the characteristics model also provides a unifying framework for analysing both financial intermediation and the process of financial innovation. We show that the role of the financial intermediary is to buy-in the primary liabilities of firms and other organisations in financial deficit, unbundle and repackage the characteristics contained in them, and issue a set of ultimate assets that sectors in financial surplus, such as households, prefer to hold. Assets exist because the balance between the demand for and supply of asset characteristics indicates an interior equilibrium. Financial innovations arise whenever changes in demand and supply induce movements from a corner solution to the interior. Financial innovations occur as a process over time and we examine the role of external factors, such as the business cycle and changes in technology, constraints and regulations, in influencing this process. Most existing theories concentrate either on the supply side of the innovation process or on the demand side; we show in this chapter how these existing explanations can be integrated in the characteristics model.

Chapter 4 (originally published as Heffernan, 1990a; see also Heffernan, 1990b) employs the characteristics approach to both define and classify financial products and markets. A simple model with three characteristics is used, the three characteristics being expected return, security (as measured by the spread between maximum and minimum returns) and liquidity (as measured by the time or cost of converting a financial product into an acceptable medium of exchange). With three characteristics, a three-dimensional efficiency frontier can be constructed. The model is then used to define two classes of financial product: (a) those that contain one or more of the three characteristics and are held in investor portfolios either as assets or as liabilities, and (b) those that enable the characteristics combination of the current portfolio to be altered. The first category contains all the familiar assets held by investors. For example, current accounts will plot on the efficiency frontier at the point indicating very high liquidity and security but low expected return. In contrast, shares will plot at a point indicating high expected return, low security and with high liquidity, but less than that offered by current accounts. Property, on the other hand, has high expected return, high security and low liquidity. The second category contains portfolio management products, such as options, forwards and swaps; these can be used, for example, to increase the security (i.e. reduce the risk) of the current portfolio by reducing the exposure of the portfolio to interest rate or exchange rate risk.

The model is then used to analyse the impact of regulatory and technological changes in the financial markets, with special reference to the reforms in the UK stock market in the 1980s, namely the deregulations known as 'Big Bang' and the Financial Services Act of 1986, and the introduction in 1989 of a new technology known as SAEF, a system that automatically executes small orders to buy and sell marketable securities at the best prices. At the same time, the spread of information technology was improving the speed of information flows on a global level. We show that one effect of these changes, by reducing transactions costs and increasing competition between market makers, was to raise the expected returns (net of costs) and improve the liquidity of marketable securities traded on the London Stock Exchange. However, faster information flows tend to increase price volatility and hence reduce security; this became especially clear after the October 1987 crash. The overall effect of these regulatory and technological changes, therefore, was to increase the quantity embodied in the marketable securities of two characteristics and reduce the quantity of the third. This has moved the locus of marketable securities on the efficiency frontier and induced a change in demand relative to other financial products. Whether the demand for particular marketable securities rises or falls depends on the balance between the rise and fall in the amounts of the three characteristics embodied in each security.

Chapter 5 (originally published as Heffernan, 1992) argues that the nonprice characteristics of a financial product are as important as its price. For example, in banking, characteristics such as the number of branches, number of automated teller machines, service charges, minimum investment amount, minimum deposit amount, minimum cheque amount, maximum withdrawal amount per week, period of notice before making a withdrawal, and number of times interest is paid per year are important components of the retail product (such as interest-bearing chequing accounts or deposit accounts) offered to customers. Similarly, with repayment mortgages or personal loans, important nonprice characteristics are the degree of security provided by the borrower as insurance against the possibility of default, the minimum and maximum sizes of the sum borrowed, and the minimum and maximum terms. In order to measure the competitive stance of different banks and other providers of similar products, it is essential both to price these characteristics and then to make appropriate adjustments to the price of the product sold. This can be achieved by computing the 'interest equivalences' or the 'implicit interest' of the nonprice characteristics. To do this, Heffernan runs regression equations of the quoted interest rate for a particular product on its nonprice characteristics plus some other explanatory variables such as the absolute level of interest rates (as represented by LIBOR). The regression coefficients on the nonprice characteristics are used to compute the interest equivalences. The interest equivalence is defined as the interest earned (forgone) because of the presence of a nonprice characteristic that is, from the customer's viewpoint, negative (positive).

The model was applied to a data set on the nonprice characteristics listed above and collected by a London clearing bank on four products: higher interest chequing accounts, higher interest deposit accounts, repayment mortgages and personal loans. The following nonprice characteristics were found to be statistically important: minimum investment and deposit amounts, maximum withdrawal amount, number of branches and ATM outlets, frequency with which interest is paid, and the provision of a chequing facility. The advantage of the characteristics approach, in this context, is that it enables a more accurate measure of the 'true' price of retail banking products to be computed, and therefore enables both customers and the banks themselves to assess more accurately the benefit/cost of these products.

Chapter 6 (originally published as Desai and Low, 1987) uses the characteristics model to address the question: what are the reasons that motivate the suppliers of financial services to innovate? Desai and Low point to the explosion of new financial instruments that individuals could invest in during the 1980s, such as indexed bonds, NOW deposits, cheque-save accounts, and money market accounts. They also point to the emergence over the same period of brand-new financial institutions which began to supply instruments or services not already provided by existing institutions, such as the entry of nonbanking and even nonfinancial institutions into the financial services market, e.g. travel agencies, credit card companies and more recently retail sector companies such as Marks and Spencer, and Virgin. They argue that these developments can be explained in terms of the characteristics model, with both existing and new institutions seeking profit opportunities by searching for profitable 'gaps' in asset-characteristics space.

Desai and Low test this hypothesis using data on short-term financial products collected from the family finance page of the Saturday edition of *The Times* newspaper; this page publishes information on financial products of interest to retail customers in the UK. The products are grouped under four principal suppliers: banks, building societies, National Savings, and money market funds. They are also grouped according to six characteristics: rate of return, gross or net of tax, frequency of interest payments, access or required period of notice (e.g. 7 days, 30 days, 90 days, 180 days, annual), minimum withdrawal amount, and penalties on early withdrawal. The authors concentrate on just two of these characteristics, return net of tax and access in terms of days' notice. This enables them to construct two-dimensional graphs with the two characteristics measured along the axes and the different products depicted as vectors indicating different amounts and combinations of the two characteristics. The efficiency frontier can be constructed by means of straight lines linking up the longest vectors in two-dimensional space. They notice that some assets lie inside the efficiency frontier and so appear to be inefficient; but this may be due to the fact that the analysis is being conducted in terms of just two rather than the full set of six characteristics, so that these products have compensating amounts of other characteristics.

The authors also notice that over their sample period (January 1982 to December 1984) the number of different types of product available to retail customers increases month by month, so that there is constant innovation over the period, although it is by no means smooth, with spells of innovative activity followed by periods of inactivity. This means that each succeeding graph contains more vectors, as 'gaps' in asset-characteristics space are 'filled'. Sometimes these new vectors are close to existing vectors: the authors call this an example of 'trivial' financial innovation. Sometimes the new vectors are some distance from the existing vectors, suggesting more significant innovation. There is also evidence of 'leader' and 'follower' activity. At the beginning of the sample period, banks and building societies provided broadly similar products which were concentrated mainly at the long (one year) and short (immediate access) ends of the maturity spectrum, and there was a big gap in the middle. Competition came first from National Savings and then more seriously from money market funds. For example, National Savings began to compete at the long end with the introduction of Income and Deposit Bonds. Similarly, there was a gap between the 7-day and 30-day products and this gap was filled by money market funds offering higher yields at the 7-day end of the spectrum. Leader funds then began to fill the middle-range gap, and follower funds subsequently came in with funds offering trivial differences from these. Building societies responded by offering a range of accounts in the middle. Banks were the least innovative of the four institutions and their complacency was further challenged in 1985 when building societies started to offer cheque-save accounts and electronic cash withdrawals.

Desai and Low then go on to compute the angles between neighbouring asset vectors and use the distribution of these angles to measure the depth or thinness of the market. In a deep market, with many assets competing closely with each other, all the angles will be small and so there will be a narrow distribution of the angles. If there are gaps, the distribution of the angles will be more dispersed. The evidence indicates that both the mean value of the angle and its standard deviation decline over the sample period. This confirms that the new assets are providing increasingly close substitutes for the existing assets. But this result is also consistent with many new products being trivial rather than important innovations, so that these new products do not necessarily help to fill the big gaps in asset-characteristics space. However, there is also a trend decline in the maximum angle, although there were big cycles within the trend. Now this does indicate that, over time, the big gaps are indeed being filled and that important innovations are taking place. The evidence also shows that the new products occur where there are large gaps, although by themselves large gaps do not necessarily imply large profit opportunities and there are still many new products occurring where the gaps are fairly small. Nevertheless, this simple framework can be used to identify gaps and possible profit opportunities and hence help to explain the process of financial innovation.

The characteristics framework has both strong theoretical foundations and generally gives rise to an empirical model that, because it is generally linear or at most linear-quadratic, is usually fairly easy to estimate. We show in the chapters of this book that the characteristics model is particularly suitable to different applications in finance, including portfolio behaviour, asset pricing, financial intermediation and financial innovation. We also present some empirical results that are based on data from the UK financial sector; some of the data were publicly available, while others were collected privately but were made available on condition that their source remained confidential. The potential for further research is enormous. The financial markets and the financial services industry generally generate much higher quality data than other branches of economics, yet it is the case that gaining access to that data for the purpose of independent academic scrutiny is often difficult and/or expensive. Requests to financial service providers for access to potentially very interesting data sets are still too readily turned down on the grounds of confidentiality. Yet we show in the empirical chapters in this book that some very interesting and important results can be derived from the finance data sets we have been able to access or construct, even if these are probably too small and also possibly too incomplete to undertake a complete analysis. The chapters also point out what new data would be required to test some important hypotheses. For example, Desai and Low would like to get access to market shares of assets or turnover/volume data for different products in order to determine more precisely whether the gaps that are filled are where profit opportunities are the greatest. However, once we can gain access to larger and more complete finance data sets, then even more interesting and important results can be derived using the characteristics model.

References

Blake, D. (1986). The characteristics model of portfolio behaviour. PhD Thesis. London: London School of Economics.

Blake, D. (1990). Portfolio behaviour and asset pricing in a characteristics framework. *Scottish Journal of Political Economy*, 37, 343–59.

Blake, D. (1996). Financial intermediation and financial innovation in a characteristics framework. *Scottish Journal of Political Economy*, 43, 16–31.

Boyle, J. R., Gorman, W. M. and Pudney, S. E. (1977). The demand for related goods: A progress report. In Intriligator, M. (ed) *Frontiers in Quantitative Economics*, Volume 3A. Amsterdam: North-Holland.

Cragg, J. G. and Uhler, R. S. (1970). The demand for automobiles. *Canadian Journal of Economics*, 3, 386–406.

Deaton, A. and Muellbauer, J. (1980). *Economics and Consumer Behaviour*. Cambridge: Cambridge University Press.

Desai, M. and Low, W. (1987). Measuring the opportunity for product innovation. In De Cecco, M. (ed) *Changing Money*. Oxford: Blackwell.

Gorman, W. M. (1959). The demand for fish: An application of factor analysis. Birmingham University Discussion Paper A6, August.

Gorman, W. M. (1972). A sketch for the demand for related goods. Presidential Address to the Winter Meeting of the Econometric Society, December.

Gorman, W. M. (1976). Tricks with utility functions. In Artis, M. and Nobay, R. (eds) *Essays in Economic Analysis*. Cambridge: Cambridge University Press.

Gorman, W. M. (1980). A possible procedure for analysing quality differentials in the egg market. *Review of Economic Studies*, 47, 843–56 (originally Journal Paper J-3129 of Iowa State College of Agriculture and Mechanical Arts, 1956).

Griliches, Z. (ed) (1971). *Price Indexes and Quality Change: Studies in New Methods of Measurement*. Cambridge, Mass.: Harvard University Press.

Hansen, F. (1972). *Consumer Choice Behaviour*. New York: Free Press.

Heffernan, S. A. (1990a). A characteristics definition of financial markets. *Journal of Banking and Finance*, 14, 583–609.

Heffernan, S. A. (1990b). A characteristics analysis of regulatory changes in UK financial markets. *Japan and the World Economy*, 2, 107–39.

Heffernan, S. A. (1992). A computation of interest equivalences for non-price characteristics of bank products. *Journal of Money, Credit and Banking*, 24, 162–72.

Ironmonger, D. S. (1972). *New Commodities and Consumer Behaviour*. Cambridge: Cambridge University Press.

Kane, E. J. (1972). Risk, return and equilibrium. *Journal of Finance*, 27, 61–62.

Klevmarken, A. (1977). A note on new goods and quality changes in the true cost of living index in view of Lancaster's model of consumer behaviour. *Econometrica*, 45, 163–73.

Lancaster, K. J. (1966). A new approach to consumer theory. *Journal of Political Economy*, 74, 132–57.

Lancaster, K. J. (1971). *Consumer Demand: A New Approach*. New York: Columbia University Press.

Lucas, R. E. B. (1975). Hedonic price functions. *Economic Inquiry*, 13, 157–78.

Makower, H. (1957). *Activity Analysis and the Theory of Economic Equilibrium*. London: Macmillan.

Pudney, S. E. (1980). Disaggregated demand analysis: The estimation of a class of non-linear demand systems. *Review of Economic Studies*, 47, 875–92.

Pudney, S. E. (1981a). Instrumental variable estimation of a characteristics model of demand. *Review of Economic Studies*, 48, 417–33.

Pudney, S. E. (1981b). An empirical method of approximating the separable structure of consumer preferences. *Review of Economic Studies*, 48, 561–77.

Roberts, G. S. (1975). Lancaster's new demand theory: Its application in portfolio analysis. *Journal of Economic Literature*, 13, 45.

Sharpe, W. F. (1985). *Investments*. Englewood Cliffs, NJ: Prentice-Hall.

Stone, J. R. N. (1956). *Quantity and Price Indexes in National Accounts*. Paris: Organization for European Economic Cooperation.

Tobin, J. (1958). Liquidity preference as behaviour toward risk. *Review of Economic Studies*, 26, 65–86.

Triplett, J. E. (1976). Consumer demand and characteristics of consumption goods. In Terleckyj, N. (ed) *Household Production and Consumption*. New York: National Bureau of Economic Research.

Woodside, A. G., Sheth, J. N. and Bennett, P. D. (eds) (1977). *Consumer and Individual Buying Behaviour*. New York: North-Holland.

Chapter 2

Portfolio behaviour and asset pricing in a characteristics framework

David Blake

The characteristics model provides a unifying framework for analysing both portfolio behaviour and asset pricing. We show that
assets are demanded for the characteristics embodied in them and
that this feature can be used, in conjunction with market clearing
conditions, to derive characteristics-based models of asset pricing.

2.1 Introduction

The purpose of this chapter is to examine preference-based portfolio
behaviour and asset pricing as an application of the characteristics
model of demand. There have been a few hints in the literature about
the possibility of doing this (e.g. Kane, 1972; Roberts, 1975; Sharpe,
1985), but no formal attempt to do so. This is surprising since the
characteristics model encompasses a number of existing and very
familiar models of preference-based portfolio behaviour and asset
pricing.

In Section 2.2, we derive the characteristics model of asset demand
by individuals as the outcome of a two-stage optimisation problem:
a lower-stage cost minimisation problem which establishes an
efficient production possibility frontier between assets and characteristics, and an upper-stage utility maximisation problem which
establishes the optimal demand for characteristics and the optimal
derived demand for assets. This demand depends on asset prices,
the technological relationship between assets and characteristics, and
the preferences for characteristics. By aggregating over individual

Reprinted from *Scottish Journal of Political Economy*, Vol. 37, pp. 343–59, © 1990,
with permission from Blackwell Publishers, Oxford.

demands, we derive market demands, and by combining these with market supplies, we generate the characteristics model of asset prices. In Section 2.3, we argue that a number of existing models of portfolio behaviour and asset prices are members of the class of characteristics models: the state-preference model, the parameter-preference model, the capital asset pricing model, the intertemporal capital asset pricing model and the ARCH-in-mean pricing model. We should stress at the outset that the characteristics model covers only preference-based models of portfolio behaviour and asset pricing. It therefore excludes non-preference-based models. In particular, it excludes arbitrage-free models of asset pricing (e.g. Ross, 1976 a, b, 1978), even though, under certain conditions, both types of models give rise to linear pricing rules. Section 2.4 concludes the chapter.

2.2 The characteristics model of portfolio behaviour and asset pricing

The original characteristics model was developed by Gorman (1980) (see also Makower, 1957; Lancaster, 1966; Gorman, 1976). The aim of the model is to explain the demand for a large number of closely related goods in terms of a much smaller number of characteristics that are common to those goods. For example, if the goods in question are different types of food, the relevant characteristics could be taste, nutritiousness, hunger relief, preparation time, etc. If, on the other hand, the goods happen to be assets, the characteristics could be liquidity, reversibility, divisibility, predictability of value, and prospective yield and return.[1] The individual has preferences over the characteristics embodied in the assets rather than over the assets themselves, an idea which seems particularly sensible in relation to portfolio behaviour, since utility is ultimately derived only from consumption, and assets are held not for direct consumption but rather for their contribution to

---

1 See Tobin (n.d.). 'Liquidity' is related to the time and/or cost involved in converting an asset into cash. An asset is perfectly liquid if it can be converted into cash instantaneously and without cost. 'Reversibility' is related to the loss in value incurred when an asset is bought and subsequently sold. The degree of reversibility is measured by the bid–offer spread. An asset is perfectly reversible if trading in the asset involves no bid–offer spread. Liquidity and reversibility are related but distinct aspects of the marketability of assets.

providing for consumption in the future. If it is possible to express this contribution to future consumption in terms of the characteristics of assets currently held in the portfolio, then it is possible to form preferences over those characteristics rather than over either the assets themselves or over future consumption directly, and this is a simpler problem to solve than the full intertemporal consumption-portfolio problem (see, e.g., Merton, 1969, 1971).

However, this model is a useful way of analysing behaviour only if the number of characteristics is small in relation to the number of assets and if the asset-characteristics technology, that is, the technological relationship between the amount of an asset purchased and the quantities of characteristics that it yields, is a simple one. Gorman had assumed a very simple linear form for this technology, namely that of fixed coefficients, and this allowed him to remove the restriction of dealing with a specific but nevertheless arbitrary functional form for utility. In general, however, the asset-characteristics technology may not be so simple and the corresponding generality of the utility function may not be possible.

It is possible to construct the characteristics model as the outcome of a two-stage optimisation problem: a lower-stage cost minimisation problem and an upper-stage utility maximisation problem.

The lower-stage cost minimisation problem establishes the efficient production possibility frontier between assets and characteristics, i.e. the asset-characteristics technology. Suppose that a K-order vector of characteristics, or 'outputs', z, can be 'produced' from an N-order vector of marketable assets, or 'inputs', q, with prices, p $(K < N)$. Suppose further that the characteristics, z, are not themselves marketable (which is likely to be the general case) but that implicit or shadow prices, λ, may be attached to them. The individual's aim is to minimise the cost $y = p'q$ of achieving a given vector of characteristics, subject to the technological relationship between assets and characteristics

$$z = F(q) \tag{1}$$

(the properties of $F(\cdot)$ will be discussed below). The solution is the cost function

$$y = \phi(p, z) = \underset{q}{\text{Min}} \left[p'q \text{ subject to } z = F(q) \right] \tag{2}$$

which generates the efficient production possibility frontier between characteristics and assets.

The cost function (2) has precisely the same properties as in standard theory. In particular, its partial derivatives with respect to prices give the derived demand for assets

$$q_i = \frac{\partial \phi(p,z)}{\partial p_i} = q_i(p,z) \quad i = 1, N \tag{3}$$

and its partial derivatives with respect to the characteristics vector give the characteristics shadow prices

$$\lambda_k = \frac{\partial \phi(p,z)}{\partial z_k} = \lambda_k(p,z) \quad k = 1, K. \tag{4}$$

At the lower stage, the individual minimises the cost of reaching a vector of characteristics, z, and, along the efficiency frontier, the marginal rate of transformation between pairs of characteristics is given by

$$MRT_{ij} = -\lambda_j(p,z)/\lambda_i(p,z). \tag{5}$$

This is true in general, but in the case of portfolio behaviour, it may be unnecessary for the individual to carry out this lower-stage cost minimising exercise by himself since it is possible that the market has already performed this exercise for him (this is the efficient markets hypothesis).

The upper-stage utility maximisation problem follows from the assumption that the individual has preferences over the set of asset characteristics z (which represents future consumption potential) and c (which can be thought of as representing current consumption or the characteristics of current consumption). For convenience (although this is not necessary) we will assume a utility function that is additively separable between c and z. The individual then attempts to

$$\underset{c,z}{\text{Max}} \ \bar{u}(c) + u(z) \text{ subject to } w = c + \phi(p,z) \tag{6}$$

where w is the individual's wealth. Equation (6) generally involves a non-linear budget constraint in characteristics. The first-order conditions for a maximum are

$$\lambda = \frac{\partial \bar{u}}{\partial c} \tag{7}$$

and

$$\frac{\lambda \partial \phi}{\partial z_k} = \frac{\partial u}{\partial z_k} \quad k = 1, K \tag{8}$$

which implies, with (4), that the shadow price of the kth characteristic is given by

$$\lambda_k = \frac{1}{\lambda} \frac{\partial u}{\partial z_k} = \lambda_k(p, z) \tag{9}$$

where λ is the marginal cost of current consumption from (7). The solution to (8) is of the form

$$z_k^* = z_k^*(p, w) \tag{10}$$

which provides the optimal holdings of characteristics, given preferences. These may be substituted into (3) to give the optimal derived demand for the set of assets which contain the characteristics, namely

$$q_i^* = q_i^* [p, z^*(p, w)]. \tag{11}$$

An equivalent formulation is to optimise directly with respect to c and q:

$$\underset{c,q}{\text{Max}} \ \bar{u}(c) + u(z) \text{ subject to } w = c + p'q \text{ and } z = F(q). \tag{12}$$

This now involves a linear budget constraint in assets. The characteristics model is given by the first-order conditions for a maximum, namely

$$p_i = \sum_k^K \left(\frac{1}{\lambda} \frac{\partial u}{\partial z_k} \right) \left(\frac{\partial F_k(q)}{\partial q_i} \right)$$

$$= \sum_k^K \lambda_k(p, z) f_{ki}(q). \tag{13}$$

Equation (13) is the optimal portfolio selection equation for a particular individual. If the asset-characteristics technology or the structure of preferences is at all complicated, an explicit solution for q may not exist within (13), although if it does it will be of the form

(11). Nevertheless, (13) provides, at least implicitly, the optimal demand for assets, given prices, characteristics, preferences for characteristics (as embodied in the shadow prices of characteristics λ_k), and the asset-characteristics technology (as embodied in the terms $f_{ki}(q) = \partial F_k / \partial q_i$). Equation (13) is amenable to empirical investigation assuming that a functional form for f_{ki} can be determined and that the characteristics can be measured. The significance of the kth characteristic in determining portfolio behaviour reduces to a test of the significance of the 'regression coefficient' λ_k.

Equation (13) can also be used to examine how the optimal holding of assets changes if any of these factors changes. For example, it is possible for the introduction of a new asset to drive out an existing asset because it has a preferred set of characteristics and is introduced at a lower price than the existing asset. Similarly, it is possible for changes to the asset-characteristics technology to lead to the introduction of new assets because they can now be introduced at lower cost than before. These are examples of financial innovations and the characteristics model is particularly useful for examining financial innovations (see Chapter 3).

Equation (13) is valid for a typical individual (denoted h out of a population sized H). In general it depends on individual preferences as embodied in λ_k^h, on individual assessments of asset characteristics and (nonlinearly) on individual asset demands as reflected in $f_{ki}^h(q^h)$. As such we are, in general, unable to derive a tractable market equilibrium solution using (13). A tractable solution is possible, however, if we still allow distinct preferences but assume that the asset-characteristics technology is common to all individuals and, in addition, is either linear or quadratic.[2] This implies that the terms $f_{ki}(q^h)$ are either constant (and so independent of q^h) or are at most linear functions of q^h. If we assume that only f_{Ki} depends on q^h, then (13) becomes

$$p_i = \sum_k^{K-1} \lambda_k^h f_{ki} + \lambda_K^h f_{Ki}(q^h)$$

$$= \sum_k^{K-1} \lambda_k^h f_{ki} + \lambda_K^h \sum_j^N f_{Kij} q_j^h \qquad (14)$$

2 This assumption is the same as that for the standard capital asset pricing model (see Section 2.3 below and, e.g., Fama, 1976).

where f_{ki} and $f_{Kij} = \partial f_{Ki}/\partial q_j^h$ are constants. In this form, an explicit and unique solution for q_i exists if $f_{Kij} \neq 0$. Aggregating (14) over H individuals, and using the market-clearing conditions

$$\sum_h^H q_j^h = \bar{q}_j \quad j = 1, N \tag{15}$$

(where $\bar{q}_j$ is the market supply of the jth asset), gives

$$p_i = \sum_k^{K-1} \bar{\lambda}_k f_{ki} + \bar{\lambda}_K g_{Ki} \tag{16}$$

where

$$\bar{\lambda}_k = \bar{\lambda}_K \sum_h^H \frac{\lambda_k^h}{\lambda_K^h} \tag{17}$$

$$\bar{\lambda}_K = \left[\sum_h^H \left(\frac{1}{\lambda_K^h} \right) \right]^{-1} \tag{18}$$

and

$$g_{Ki} = \sum_j^N f_{Kij} \bar{q}_j. \tag{19}$$

To eliminate the $K\ \bar{\lambda}_k$ from (16), we employ (16) to form a system of K equations, using K assets or portfolios, one of which can be the market portfolio. We then invert the system (a typical element of the matrix inverse being γ^{jk}) and solve for the $\bar{\lambda}_k$ as

$$\bar{\lambda}_k = \sum_j^{K-1} \gamma^{kj} p_j + \gamma^{kK} p_M \tag{20}$$

where p_M is the current price of the market portfolio. These can then be eliminated from (16) to give

$$p_i = \sum_k^{K-1} \beta_{ik} p_k + \beta_{iK} p_M \quad i \neq k \tag{21}$$

where

$$\beta_{ik} = \sum_{j}^{K-1} \gamma^{jk} f_{ji} + \gamma^{Kk} g_{Ki} \qquad (22)$$

and

$$\beta_{iK} = \sum_{j}^{K-1} \gamma^{jK} f_{ji} + \gamma^{KK} g_{Ki}. \qquad (23)$$

Equation (21) is the equilibrium capital asset pricing equation for the characteristics model, under the assumptions of a common assessment of characteristics and a relationship between assets and characteristics that is either linear or quadratic. It can also be used for forecasting asset prices or for pricing new financial products (see, e.g., Chapter 3). In addition, (21) forms the basis of a K-fund separation theorem in which all optimal asset holdings can be constructed from at most K mutual funds, one of which can be the market portfolio and one the riskless asset, since any wealth not held in the other funds must be held in the riskless asset. We will examine the criteria for selecting the remaining $K - 2$ funds in Section 2.3 (see, e.g., Merton, 1973; Breeden, 1979).

Another important feature of the pricing model (21) is linearity. The linearity follows from the assumption that f_{Ki} is a linear function of q^h. Arbitrage-free models (Ross, 1976 a, b, 1978) also give rise to linear pricing rules similar to (21). But the two pricing models have entirely different origins. With the characteristics model, the β_{ik} are functions of individual preference parameters, whereas with the arbitrage-free model, the β_{ik} are preference-free loadings. Ross (1978) puts the presence of nonlinearities in asset pricing down to the existence of monopoly power in financial markets. In the characteristics model, such nonlinearities result from nonlinearity in the underlying asset-characteristics technology.

Finally, we note that since (21) has the form of a linear regression equation, it is amenable to empirical investigation. We simply regress asset prices on the prices of the K assets or portfolios used to eliminate the $\bar{\lambda}_k$. The acceptability of the model depends on how close the 'regression coefficients' β_{ik} and β_{iK} are to their theoretical values (22) and (23).

2.3   The characteristics model as a unifying framework for analysing portfolio behaviour and asset pricing

In this section, we demonstrate how the characteristics model (13) (or (14)) and (21) provides a unifying framework for analysing preference-based portfolio behaviour and asset pricing. A number of familiar models can be interpreted as members of the class of characteristics models.

2.3.1   The state-preference model

The 'state-preference' model (SPM) (see Arrow, 1964, 1965) assumes that states-of-nature determine the consequences (e.g. payoffs) of actions (e.g. portfolio decisions) that an individual may make. The payoff function, $w_s = w(s, q)$ is the payoff (e.g. value of wealth) in state s ($s = 1, S$), when portfolio decision q is taken. If the individual forms preferences over the contingent payoffs, his utility function is written as

$$u = u(w_1, \ldots, w_s) \tag{24}$$

and his objective is to choose the portfolio q to maximise (24) subject to initial wealth, w, and prices, p.

The SPM is consistent with the expected utility model (EUM) (Bernoulli, 1954; von Neumann and Morgenstern, 1944), since a special case of (24) is

$$u = \sum_{s=1}^{S} f_s u(w_s) \tag{25}$$

where the f_s are non-negative numbers which can be chosen to sum to unity and where the $u(.)$s are simply sub-utility functions of the general form. If we interpret the f_s as the probabilities of different states occurring, the parallel with expected utility is valid.

Suppose that there are N assets q_i with initial prices p_i, and state-contingent prices p_{is} (i.e. number of dollars delivered in state s by the ith asset), so that the payoff in state s from choosing portfolio q is $w_s = \sum_{i}^{N} p_{is} q_i$, then the first-order conditions for an optimum are

$$p_i = \sum_{s=1}^{S} \left(\frac{f_s}{\lambda} \frac{\partial u}{\partial w_s} \right) p_{is} = \sum_{s=1}^{S} \lambda_s p_{is} \quad i = 1, N. \tag{26}$$

Here λ_s is the Arrow–Debreu price or shadow price of the payoff if state s occurs.

It is clear how the SPM can be interpreted as a characteristics model with (26) having the same structure as (13). The states s (or payoffs in different states) are equivalent to the characteristics z and the payoff functions $w(s, q)$ are equivalent to the asset-characteristics technology, $g(z, q) = z - F(q)$. Therefore, the objects of choice in the characteristics model, namely the characteristics, are equivalent to the objects of choice in the SPM, namely the payoffs. All assets have different characteristics since they all have different payoffs in different states of nature.

2.3.2 The parameter-preference model

The '*parameter-preference*' model (PPM) was originally formulated as a two-parameter model by Markowitz (1952, 1959) and Tobin (1958, 1966). A generalised version of the two-parameter model has been developed by Fishburn (1977). The PPM greatly simplified the problem of uncertainty by assuming that each individual forms preferences over different portfolios which depend on only a small number of parameters relating to the distribution of asset prices.

Fishburn (1977) considered a version of the two-parameter PPM called the 'mean-risk preference' model. It depends on two parameters of the portfolio, namely a 'mean function' which is defined on the distribution function as

$$m(F) = \int_{-\infty}^{\gamma(F)} w dF(w) \tag{27}$$

and a 'risk function' (taken from Stone, 1973) which is defined on the distribution function as

$$v(F) = \int_{-\infty}^{\gamma(F)} |w - \mu(F)|^\alpha dF(w) \quad \alpha \geq 0 \tag{28}$$

where $\mu(F)$ is the reference level-of-wealth parameter from which deviations are measured, with these deviations rescaled by a non-negative parameter α, and where $\gamma(F)$ is the upper-range parameter. The individual forms preferences over the mean and risk functions for different portfolios and these preferences depend on at most three parameters relating to the distribution, namely $\mu(F)$, $\gamma(F)$ and α.

There are a number of interesting and familiar special cases of the mean-risk preference model.

1   The '*mean-variance preference*' *model (MVPM)*. This is the seminal PPM of Markowitz (1952, 1959) which sets $\gamma(F) = \infty$, $\mu(F) = m(F)$ and $\alpha = 2$. With this model an aversion to risk is equivalent to an aversion to variance. The MVPM is consistent with the EUM as long as the individual's utility function is quadratic or the distribution of asset prices is normal. The utility function takes the form $u = u(m, v)$ and the first-order conditions for a maximum are

$$p_i = \left(\frac{1}{\lambda}\frac{\partial u}{\partial m}\right)\frac{\partial m}{\partial q_i} + \left(\frac{1}{\lambda}\frac{\partial u}{\partial v}\right)\frac{\partial v}{\partial q_i} = \lambda_m \mu_i + \lambda_v \sum_j^N \sigma_{ij} q_j \quad (29)$$

where μ_i is the expected price of the ith asset and σ_{ij} is the covariance between the prices of the ith and jth assets.

2   The '*below mean semi-variance preference*' *model*. This sets $\gamma(F) = \mu(F) = m(F)$ and $\alpha = 2$ and so defines risk as a probability-weighted function of deviations below the mean return on the portfolio. The first-order conditions for a maximum are as in (29) except that v is defined as a semi-variance and σ_{ij} defined as a semi-covariance.

3   The '*target semi-variance preference*' *model (TSVPM)*. This sets $\gamma(F) = \mu(F) = \tau$ and $\alpha = 2$ and so defines risk as a probability-weighted function of deviations below a given target return τ; that is, risk is associated with failure to achieve a target return. The first-order conditions for a maximum are as in (29) except that m, μ_i, v and σ_{ij} are defined with respect to the target τ.

4   The 'α–τ' *model*. This is the most general of the mean-risk preference models. It involves target returns and allows α to take values other than 2. If $\alpha = 0$, the risk measure is simply the probability of failing to get the target return (equivalent to the 'safety-first' model of Roy, 1952). The worst possible outcome is represented by $\alpha = \infty$. In the α–τ model, the individual is free to choose both α and τ. For example, τ can be selected as the bankruptcy level of returns, the zero-profit return (i.e. no gain–no loss) or the riskless rate. Again the first-order conditions are similar to (29), but in this case both μ_i and σ_{ij} depend on α and τ.

Each of these four versions of the PPM is consistent with the characteristics model, with the different characteristics being the different versions of the mean and risk functions and λ_m and λ_v being the shadow prices of those characteristics. Equation (29) has the same structure as (14) when $K = 2$, and this follows because the asset-characteristics technologies in the two models are similar. They both have one characteristic which is linearly related to assets (via the mean function in (29)) and one which is quadratically related to assets (via the risk function in (29)).

2.3.3   The capital asset pricing model

The 'capital asset pricing' model (CAPM) of Sharpe (1964) and Lintner (1965) is a market equilibrium parameter preference model. There are now several versions of the model and we will consider three of them.

1   *The original two-parameter CAPM with homogeneous expectations.* The original model assumes that individuals are concerned with only two parameters of the portfolio, namely expected return and risk, and that they have homogeneous expectations. It is derived from an individual optimisation strategy equivalent to that in the MVPM. It then aggregates over individuals, imposes market clearing and uses side conditions to eliminate unobservables. The resulting model takes the form (see Fama, 1976, pp. 305–13)

$$p_i = \lambda_1 \mu_i + \lambda_2 \beta_{iM} \tag{30}$$

where

$$\lambda_1 = \frac{1}{1 + R_0}, \quad \lambda_2 = \frac{-(\mu_M - (1 + R_0)p_M)}{1 + R_0} \tag{31}$$

and

$$\beta_{iM} = \frac{\sigma_{iM}}{\sigma_M^2}. \tag{32}$$

In (31), R_0 is the risk-free rate of interest, p_M is the current value of the market portfolio, and μ_M is the expected value of the market portfolio at the end of the period. In (32), β_{iM} is the beta factor for the ith asset defined as the ratio of the ith asset's covariance with the market portfolio to the variance of the market portfolio.

The interpretation of (30) is that in an efficient market, each asset (and therefore the current price of each asset) embodies two components: an expected market value at the end of the period, μ_i, and the risk attached to that value at the end of the period, β_{iM}. The price of a unit of expected value is λ_1 and the price of a unit of risk (or the risk premium) is λ_2.

2   *The two-parameter CAPM with heterogeneous expectations.* The model in (30) assumes homogeneous expectations by individuals. But this assumption is not necessary for market equilibrium. Market equilibrium merely requires that the p_i are the market clearing prices at the beginning of the period. The problem, however, is that the resulting pricing equations contain parameters that cannot be estimated from observed data. The equation corresponding to (30) in the case of heterogeneous expectations is (see Fama, 1976, pp. 314–19)

$$p_i = \lambda_1 \mu_i' + \lambda_2' \beta_{iM}' \tag{33}$$

where

$$\lambda_1 = \frac{1}{1 + R_0}, \quad \lambda_2' = \frac{-(\mu_M' - (1 + R_0)p_M)}{1 + R_0} \tag{34}$$

and

$$\mu_i' = \frac{\sum\limits_{h}^{H} \alpha^h \mu_i^h}{\sum\limits_{h}^{H} \alpha^h}, \quad \beta_{iM}' = \frac{\sum\limits_{h}^{H} \sigma_{iw}^h}{\sum\limits_{h}^{H} \sigma_{Mw}^h} \tag{35}$$

and

$$\alpha^h = \frac{\partial v^h}{\partial m^h}, \quad \sigma_{iw}^h = \sum\limits_{j}^{N} \sigma_{ij}^h q_j^h, \tag{36}$$

where σ_{iw}^h is the ith asset's covariance with individual h's portfolio. Equation (33) has the same form as (30) and μ_i', λ_2' and β_{iM}' have the same interpretation as μ_i, λ_2 and β_{iM}. When there are identical expectations (33) reduces to (30). However, in general, μ_i', λ_2' and β_{iM}' cannot be inferred from observed data since they depend on individual assessments.

3   *The K-parameter CAPM with homogeneous expectations.* The original CAPM assumed that individuals were concerned only with risk and return. In reality they are concerned with many other factors. In general, with K factors or parameters, the CAPM will be a K-dimensional hyperplane. In an efficient market, all assets will be represented by points on the hyperplane.

Sharpe (1985) considers one example of an additional factor, namely reversibility. The reversibility properties of assets (i.e. the cost of buying and selling assets, or their bid–offer spread)[3] are positive attributes of assets. When reversibility, ℓ_i, is taken into account, the CAPM takes the form

$$p_i = \lambda_1\mu_i + \lambda_2\beta_{iM} + \lambda_3\ell_i. \tag{37}$$

In an efficient market, (37) describes a security market hyperplane. For given risk, the greater the reversibility of the asset, the lower the expected price. For given expected price, the greater the risk, the greater the reversibility has to be.

Brennan (1970) and Litzenberger and Ramaswamy (1979) consider another example. They argue that because of differential taxes, individuals may prefer capital gains to dividends. Brennan proposed a version of the CAPM that accounted for the taxation of dividends. With proportional individual tax rates, the CAPM takes the form

$$p_i = \lambda_1\mu_i + \lambda_2\beta_{iM} + \lambda_3 D_i \tag{38}$$

where

$$\lambda_1 = \frac{1}{1 + R_0(1 - \tau)}$$

$$\lambda_2 = \frac{-(\mu_M - (1 + R_0(1 - \tau))p_M - \tau D_M)}{1 + R_0(1 - \tau)}$$

$$\lambda_3 = \frac{-\tau}{1 + R_0(1 - \tau)}. \tag{39}$$

---

3 Sharpe actually calls this liquidity, but in line with Tobin's nomenclature we will call it reversibility.

D_i and D_M are the dividends on the ith asset and market portfolio respectively, and τ is a positive coefficient that accounts for the taxation of dividends and interest as income and the taxation of capital gains at a preferential rate. Litzenberger and Ramaswamy extend Brennan's model to account for progressive taxation but the principle is the same, namely that an increase in τ makes high-dividend assets less attractive to individuals and so reduces the equilibrium price of such assets.

We have discussed three versions of the CAPM and we can see immediately how they fit into the framework of the market equilibrium version of the characteristics model given by (21). The β_{ik} in (21) (which depend on f_{ki}, the ith asset's embodiment of the kth characteristic from (13)) correspond to the parameters (e.g. μ_i, β_{iM}, ℓ_i) of the CAPM (which measure the ith asset's embodiment of expected return, market risk and reversibility) and the p_k in (21) (which depend on λ_k, the shadow prices of the characteristics from (13)) correspond to the λ_k in (30), (37) or (38) which are the shadow prices of the CAPM's parameters. The mean-variance efficiency frontier of the CAPM corresponds to the efficient asset-characteristics technological frontier of the characteristics model. In the latter case, the efficiency is the result of a cost-minimising exercise by the individual as the lower stage optimisation problem. In the former case, the MV efficiency is ensured by the market.

2.3.4   The intertemporal capital asset pricing model

An obvious extension of the one-period CAPM is to make the model intertemporal. Merton (1973) was the first to do this. At the same time, he allows the investment opportunities to be stochastic. Breeden (1979), in turn, modifies Merton's model to allow both consumption and investment opportunities to be stochastic. We will examine each of these models in turn.

1   *The intertemporal CAPM with stochastic investment opportunities.* Merton develops the model in continuous time with the state variables driven by contemporaneously correlated stochastic processes of the Ito type. The state variables are the current level of wealth $w(t)$ and a vector $x(t)$ which characterises the changing investment opportunities facing the individual. The $(K-2)$-order vector $x(t)$ contains the current

values of asset prices (p_i), the expected asset prices (μ_i) and the standard deviations of asset prices (σ_i). We can define $J[w(t), x(t), t]$ as the indirect utility function of wealth showing the maximum expected utility between the current period t and the individual's death at T, assuming that an optimal policy is followed from t onwards. Using Bellman's principle of optimality, Merton shows that at each point in time, $J[.]$ satisfies the following second-order partial differential system:

$$0 = \underset{c,q}{\text{Max}} \left\{ \bar{u}(c,t) + \left[J_w m + J_t + \sum_k^{K-2} J_k n_k + \frac{1}{2} J_{ww} v \right. \right.$$
$$\left. \left. + \sum_k^{K-2} \sum_i^N J_{kw} \eta_{ik} q_i + \frac{1}{2} \sum_k^{K-2} \sum_\ell^{K-2} J_{k\ell} S_{k\ell} \right] \right\} \qquad (40)$$

where

$$m = \sum_i^N [\mu_i - (1 + R_0)p_i]q_i + (R_0 w - c) \qquad (41)$$

is the expected value of the portfolio,

$$v = \sum_i^N \sum_j^N \sigma_{ij} q_i q_j \qquad (42)$$

is the variance of the portfolio, σ_{ij} is the covariance between the ith and jth asset prices, n_k is the expected value of the kth element of the state vector $x(t)$, $S_{k\ell}$ is the covariance between the kth and ℓth elements of $x(t)$ and η_{ik} is the covariance between the ith price and kth element of $x(t)$.

The first-order conditions are derived from (40):

$$0 = \bar{u}_c - J_w \qquad (43)$$

$$0 = J_w[\mu_i - (1 + R_0)p_i] + J_{ww} \sum_j^N \sigma_{ij} q_j + \sum_k^{K-2} J_{kw} \eta_{ik}$$
$$i = 1, N. \quad (44)$$

Equation (43) is the intertemporal envelope condition equating the marginal utility of current consumption to the marginal utility of wealth (future consumption) (cf. (7)).

Asset demands are determined by inverting (44):

$$q_i = T_w \sum_j^N \sigma^{ij}[\mu_i - (1 + R_0)p_i] + \sum_k^{K-2} T_k \sum_j^N \sigma^{ij}\eta_{jk} \qquad (45)$$

where $\{\sigma^{ij}\} = \{\sigma_{ij}\}^{-1}$, $T_w = -J_w/J_{ww}$ is the individual's absolute risk tolerance defined on wealth and $T_k = -J_{kw}/J_{ww}$. There are two components to the demand for assets. The first is the conventional demand by an individual with single-period mean-variance preferences. The second is the hedging demand against adverse shifts in the investment opportunity set: $T_k \sum_j^N \sigma^{ij}\eta_{jk}$ is the demand for asset i to hedge against the adverse effect of the state variable x_k acting through its covariance with p_i.

Merton (1973) shows that the $K - 2$ hedging factors give rise to generalised separation based on K mutual funds. All individuals, regardless of preferences, can construct portfolios based on at most K funds: the riskless asset, the market portfolio and $K - 2$ portfolios having the highest correlations with the $K - 2$ state variables, given by $\sum_j^N \sigma^{ij}\eta_{jk}$, $k = 1, K - 2$.

Finally, it is possible to derive the intertemporal CAPM in the same way as the CAPM for the characteristics model was derived in (14) to (21):

$$p_i = \lambda_1\mu_i + \lambda_2\beta_{iM} + \sum_k^{K-2} \lambda_k\beta_{ik} \qquad (46)$$

where λ_1 and λ_2 are given by (31), and

$$\lambda_k = \frac{-(\mu_k - (1 + R_0)p_k)}{1 + R_0} \qquad (47)$$

$$\beta_{iM} = \sigma_{iM}\gamma^{11} - \sum_j^{K-2} \eta_{ij}\gamma^{j+1.1} \qquad (48)$$

$$\beta_{ik} = \sigma_{iM}\gamma^{1,k+1} - \sum_j^{K-2} \eta_{ij}\gamma^{j+1,k+1} \qquad (49)$$

where γ^{jk} has the same interpretation as in (22) and (23).

Equation (46) is the multi($K - 1$)-beta version of Merton's intertemporal CAPM. In equilibrium and assuming homogeneous expectations, individuals are compensated in terms of expected return for bearing systematic (market) risk and for bearing the risk of unfavourable shifts in $K - 2$ investment opportunities. It therefore falls neatly into the characteristics framework with the $K - 2$ state variables being interpreted as characteristics to which the asset portfolio responds, the portfolio's embodiment of the kth characteristic being $\sum_i^N J_{kw} \eta_{ik} q_i$.

2 *The intertemporal CAPM with stochastic investment and consumption opportunities.* Breeden accepts Merton's framework given by (43) and (44) but argues that in practice it is difficult to identify the $K - 2$ state variables characterising stochastic investment opportunities. He also argues that it is unnecessary because the multi-beta model can be shown to be equivalent to a single-beta model defined with respect to aggregate consumption rather than the state variables, since the correlation between asset prices and aggregate consumption is a more appropriate measure of risk than the correlation between asset prices and aggregate wealth. When consumption opportunities are stochastic, consumption has the form $c = c[w(t), x(t), t]$.

From (43) we have

$$J_{ww} = \overline{u}_{cc} c_w$$
$$J_{wk} = \overline{u}_{cc} c_k \tag{50}$$

where $c_w = \partial c / \partial w$, $c_k = \partial c / \partial x_k$. Substituting (50) into (44) and rearranging gives (using (36))

$$T_c(\mu_i - (1 + R_0)p_i) = \sigma_{iw} c_w + \sum_k^K \eta_{ik} c_k \tag{51}$$

where $T_c = -\overline{u}_c / \overline{u}_{cc}$ is the individual's absolute risk tolerance defined on consumption. But from $c[w, x, t]$ we have

$$dc = c_w dw + \sum_k^K c_k dx_k \tag{52}$$

so that changes in consumption are linearly related to changes in wealth and the state variables. Multiplying each side of (52) by p_i and taking expectations gives

$$\sigma_{ic} = \sigma_{iw}c_w + \sum_k^K \eta_{ik}c_k \tag{53}$$

which is identical to the right-hand side of (51). This shows that the optimal portfolio is chosen so that the covariance of each asset price with optimal consumption is proportional to the asset's expected excess return.

Again we can derive the intertemporal CAPM in this case to be

$$p_i = \lambda_1 \mu_i + \lambda_2 \beta_{ic} \tag{54}$$

where

$$\lambda_1 = \frac{1}{1 + R_0}, \quad \lambda_2 = \frac{-(\mu_M - (1 + R_0)p_M)}{\beta_{Mc}(1 + R_0)} \tag{55}$$

and

$$\beta_{ic} = \frac{\sigma_{ic}}{\sigma_c^2}, \quad \beta_{Mc} = \frac{\sigma_{Mc}}{\sigma_c^2} \tag{56}$$

are the consumption betas of asset i and the market portfolio respectively.

Breeden's main argument is that in equilibrium, an asset's risk can be represented by a single beta with respect to aggregate consumption and this is 'a considerable simplification over the Merton multi-beta derivation, at no loss of generality in assumptions' (1979, p. 276). The higher an asset's beta with respect to consumption, the more attractive the asset and the higher its equilibrium expected return. The model (54) is clearly a characteristics model, with the principal risk characteristic being an asset's correlation with aggregate consumption.

2.3.5 The ARCH-in-mean pricing model

The ARCH-in-mean (ARCH-M) pricing model takes the form (see Engle, Lilien and Robins, 1987):

$$p_{it} = \lambda_1 \mu_{it} + \lambda_2 \sigma_t^2 + u_t \tag{57}$$

where

$$\lambda_1 = \frac{1}{1 + R_0}, \quad \lambda_2 = \frac{-(\mu_M - (1 + R_0)p_M)}{1 + R_0} \tag{58}$$

and

$$\sigma_t^2 = \omega_0 + \sum_{i=1}^{q} \omega_{1i} u_{t-i}^2. \tag{59}$$

The expressions in (58) are identical to those in (31). Equation (57) explains the conditional mean price, μ_{it}, of the ith asset at the end of period t, in terms of the conditional variance, σ_t^2, of the price of the ith asset and an unforecastable 'news' term, u_t, which has a zero conditional expected value at the beginning of period t. The conditional variance is defined in (59) as the one-period ahead forecast variance, conditional on information up to time t. The information in this case is 'news' concerning the asset's price volatility during the previous q periods. These are defined as q lags of the squared residuals from the conditional mean equation, $u_{t-1}^2, \ldots, u_{t-q}^2$.

Equation (59) is an ARCH(q) model, where ARCH stands for autoregressive conditional heteroscedasticity. This follows because the conditional variance of the asset price depends on an autoregressive component (the lags of the squared residuals) and this will render the conditional variance heteroscedastic or time-varying. ARCH models were devised by Engle (1982) and have wide applications in financial econometrics (see, e.g., Bollerslev, Chou and Kroner, 1992; Bollerslev, Engle and Nelson, 1994).

The ARCH model was generalised by Bollerslev (1986) as GARCH (generalised ARCH). The GARCH (p, q) model for the conditional variance takes the form

$$\sigma_t^2 = \omega_0 + \sum_{i=1}^{q} \omega_{1i} u_{t-i}^2 + \sum_{j=1}^{p} \omega_{2j} \sigma_{t-j}^2 \tag{60}$$

and involves q ARCH terms and p GARCH terms involving lags of the conditional variance itself. The ARCH (q) model is a special case of the GARCH (p, q) model in which $p = 0$. The advantage of the GARCH model is that a low-order GARCH model often works as well or indeed better than a high-order ARCH model, so that fewer parameters need to be estimated. The most common form of the GARCH model is the GARCH $(1,1)$:

$$\sigma_t^2 = \omega_0 + \omega_1 u_{t-1}^2 + \omega_2 \sigma_{t-1}^2. \tag{61}$$

In (61), the variance of the asset price in period t is predicted from three components: a long-term average estimate of the variance (ω_0), news on the price volatility observed in the previous period (the ARCH term) and the forecasted variance from the previous period (the GARCH term). If the asset price was unexpectedly high or low in the previous period, then the forecast of the variance in the subsequent period will be raised. The model can therefore explain the volatility clustering that is observed in the prices of financial assets, whereby large price changes are likely to be followed by further large price changes.

The parallels between (57) and (30) are clear with the conditional variance in (57) providing an alternative risk characteristic to the unconditional beta factor in (30).

2.4 Conclusion

We have applied the characteristics model to the problem of portfolio behaviour and asset pricing. By defining assets in terms of characteristics, we generated individual demands for assets which depended on the prices of assets, the technological relationship between assets and asset characteristics, and the individual's preferences for different characteristics. In general, the characteristics model cannot be readily aggregated across individuals. However, when we assumed that the asset-characteristics technology had a simple form which was common to all individuals, market-clearing conditions could be used to derive an asset pricing model. Finally, we showed that the characteristics model provides a unified approach to the problem of preference-based portfolio behaviour and asset pricing. A number of existing models can be interpreted as characteristics models: the state-preference model, the parameter-preference model, the capital asset pricing model, the intertemporal capital asset pricing model and the ARCH-in-mean pricing model.

References

Arrow, K. (1964). Theory of risk aversion. In *Essays in the Theory of Risk Aversion*, Chapter 5. Amsterdam: North-Holland.

Arrow, K. (1965). *Aspects of the Theory of Risk-Bearing*. Helsinki: Yrjö Jahnsson Foundation.

Bernoulli, D. (1954). Exposition of a new theory of the measurement of risk. *Econometrica*, 22, 23–36. (Translated from Specimen theoriae novae de mensura sortis, *Papers of the Imperial Academy of Sciences in Petersburg* (1738), 5, 175–92.)

Bollerslev, T. (1986). Generalized autoregressive conditional heteroscedasticity. *Journal of Econometrics*, 31, 307–27.

Bollerslev, T., Chou, R. Y. and Kroner, K. F. (1992). ARCH modelling in finance: A review of the theory and empirical evidence. *Journal of Econometrics*, 52, 5–59.

Bollerslev, T., Engle, R. F. and Nelson, D. B. (1994). ARCH models. In *Handbook of Econometrics*, Volume 4, Chapter 49. Amsterdam: North-Holland.

Breeden, D. T. (1979). An inter-temporal asset pricing model with stochastic consumption and investment opportunities. *Journal of Financial Economics*, 7, 265–96.

Brennan, M. J. (1970). Investor taxes, market equilibrium and corporate finance. PhD Thesis. Cambridge, Mass.: MIT.

Engle, R. F. (1982). Autoregressive conditional heteroscedasticity with estimates of the variance of UK inflation. *Econometrica*, 50, 987–1008.

Engle, R. F., Lilien, D. M. and Robins, R. P. (1987). Estimating time-varying risk premia in the term structure: The ARCH-M model. *Econometrica*, 55, 391–407.

Fama, E. (1976). *Foundations of Finance*. Oxford: Blackwell.

Fishburn, P. (1977). Mean-risk analysis with risk associated with below-target returns. *American Economic Review*, 67, 116–26.

Gorman, W. M. (1976). Tricks with utility functions. In Artis, M. and Nobay, R. (eds) *Essays in Economic Analysis*. Cambridge: Cambridge University Press.

Gorman, W. M. (1980). A possible procedure for analysing quality differentials in the egg market. *Review of Economic Studies*, 47, 843–56 (originally Journal Paper J-3129 of Iowa State College of Agriculture and Mechanical Arts, 1956).

Kane, E. J. (1972). Risk, return and equilibrium. *Journal of Finance*, 27, 61–62.

Lancaster, K. J. (1966). A new approach to consumer theory. *Journal of Political Economy*, 74, 132–57.

Lintner, J. (1965). The valuation of risk assets and the selection of risky investments in stock portfolios and capital budgets. *Review of Economics and Statistics*, 47, 13–37.

Litzenberger, R. H. and Ramaswamy, K. (1979). The effect of personal taxes and dividends on capital asset prices. *Journal of Financial Economics*, 7, 163–95.

Makower, H. (1957). *Activity Analysis and the Theory of Economic Equilibrium*. London: Macmillan.

Markowitz, H. (1952). Portfolio selection. *Journal of Finance*, 7, 77–91.

Markowitz, H. (1959). *Portfolio Selection: Efficient Diversification of Investments*. Cowles Foundation for Research in Economics, Monograph 16, Yale University. New York: Wiley.

Merton, R. C. (1969). Lifetime portfolio selection under uncertainty: The continuous-time case. *Review of Economics and Statistics*, 51, 247–57.

Merton, R. C. (1971). Optimum consumption and portfolio rules in a continuous-time model. *Journal of Economic Theory*, 3, 373–413.

Merton, R. C. (1973). An inter-temporal capital asset pricing model. *Econometrica*, 41, 867–87.

Roberts, G. S. (1975). Lancaster's new demand theory: Its application in portfolio analysis. *Journal of Economic Literature*, 13, 45.

Ross, S. A. (1976a). The arbitrage theory of capital asset pricing. *Journal of Economic Theory*, 3, 343–62.

Ross, S.A. (1976b). Return, risk and arbitrage. In Friend, I. and Bicksler, J. (eds) *Risk and Return in Finance*. Cambridge, Mass.: Ballinger.

Ross, S. A. (1978). A simple approach to the valuation of risky income streams. *Journal of Business*, 51, 453–75.

Roy, A. D. (1952). Safety first and the holding of assets. *Econometrica*, 20, 431–99.

Sharpe, W. F. (1964). Capital asset prices: A theory of market equilibrium under conditions of risk. *Journal of Finance*, 19, 425–41.

Sharpe, W. F. (1985). *Investments*. Englewood Cliffs, NJ: Prentice-Hall.

Stone, B. (1973). A general class of three-parameter risk measures. *Journal of Finance*, 28, 675–85.

Tobin, J. (1958). Liquidity preference as behaviour toward risk. *Review of Economic Studies*, 26, 65–86.

Tobin, J. (1966). Theory of portfolio selection. In Hahn, F. and Brechling, F. (eds) *Theory of Interest Rates*. London: Macmillan.

Tobin, J. (n.d.) Properties of assets. Chapter 2 of unpublished manuscript.

von Neumann, J. and Morgenstern, O. (1944). *Theory of Games and Economic Behaviour*. Princeton, NJ: Princeton University Press.

Chapter 3

Financial intermediation and financial innovation in a characteristics framework

David Blake

The characteristics model provides a unifying framework for analysing both financial intermediation and the process of financial innovation. The role of the financial intermediary is to buy-in the primary liabilities of the firm, unbundle and repackage the characteristics contained in them and issue a set of ultimate assets to households. Assets exist because the balance between the supply of and demand for asset characteristics indicates an interior equilibrium. Financial innovations arise whenever changes in supply and demand induce movements from a corner solution to the interior. A number of existing explanations of financial innovation can be expressed using this framework.

The [financial] innovation process has produced many new instruments in a particular historical sequence. An ideal theory of the process should explain how changes in general economic conditions created specific profit opportunities for new instruments to emerge. It should explain all innovations and the order in which they arose and should relate to a wide range of historical experience. There is no accepted theory of innovations that meets all of these criteria. ...

It is certainly possible to describe the innovation process in very general terms. Any financial instrument can be viewed as a combination of characteristics. ... Financial innovation, then, can be seen as the process of unbundling and repackaging these characteristics to create new instruments.

The Cross Report (1986, p. 169)

Reprinted from *Scottish Journal of Political Economy*, Vol. 43, pp. 16–31, © 1996, with permission from Blackwell Publishers, Oxford.

3.1 Introduction

Any financial system has the following four components: claims, services, delivery systems and organisations. Financial intermediation and financial innovation can be associated with changes in any of these. In this chapter, we examine financial intermediation and the process of financial innovation in a characteristics framework. Claims and services are defined in terms of both internal characteristics and external characteristics, namely the delivery systems and organisations that provide them.[1] We examine: the supply of internal characteristics by primary borrowers and the demand for them by ultimate lenders; the role of financial intermediaries in unbundling and repackaging these characteristics; and the role of external factors such as the business cycle and changes in technology, constraints and regulations in influencing this process over time.

The approach that we adopt is an integrated one and examines financial innovations from both the demand side and supply side. We argue that claims and services exist because the balance between the supply of and demand for their characteristics (both internal and external) indicates an interior equilibrium, and financial innovations arise whenever changes in supply or demand induce movements from a corner solution to the interior.

Conventional explanations have typically concentrated either on the supply side of the innovation process or on the demand side. Examples of the former range from those that regard exogenous technical change as the dominant factor inducing innovation, to

---

1 The distinction between claims and services is often imprecise. While pure financial services exist, many financial services are linked to the underlying assets and are therefore part of the definition of the assets themselves. For example, a current account with a cash dispensing facility combines an asset and a service, giving a different asset from that of a current account without such a facility. In the characteristics model, however, the distinction between claims and services is not important. What is important is the configuration of characteristics embodied in the claim or service. In the above example, the current account with cash dispenser provides an additional quantity of a particular characteristic (namely liquidity) compared with that of the current account alone. Throughout the remainder of the chapter, the analysis will be conducted mainly in terms of assets. However, the framework can easily accommodate pure services. In a similar way, the distinction between delivery systems and organisations can be imprecise.

those that view innovations as being endogenous to the financial system itself, in the one case responding to constraints (or transactions costs) of various kinds (e.g. Silber, 1975, 1983; Ross, 1989), in the other responding to regulations (or taxes) of various kinds (e.g. Kane, 1981, 1983; Miller, 1986, 1991). We demonstrate how all these explanations fit into the characteristics framework and therefore how the characteristics model provides a unifying framework for analysing the process of financial innovation.

In Section 3.2, we examine financial intermediation in a characteristics framework; in Section 3.3, we develop the characteristics model of financial innovation;[2] Section 3.4 concludes.

3.2   The characteristics model of financial intermediation

Financial intermediation can be characterised very simply. Primary claims are issued by primary borrowers (typically firms) and ultimate claims are held by ultimate lenders (typically households). Intermediating between these two groups is a set of financial institutions producing intermediate claims and services. These financial intermediaries will use a variety of delivery systems to distribute and market their claims and services: branch networks, door-to-door sales forces, call centres, post, card transfers, automated teller machines, etc.

Niehans (1983) argues that all financial products are functions of three basic financial services that are immutable: the bringing together of borrowers and lenders, the exchange of money between the present and future (including contingent intertemporal transfers such as insurance), and the execution of a payments (money transmission) system. In providing these services, financial intermediaries perform three resource-using functions: the processing of information, the transformation of maturities and the provision of liquidity, and the transformation of risks (see, e.g., Benston and Smith, 1976; Greenbaum and Higgins, 1983). Each of these functions involves substantial scale economies which together justify the existence of financial intermediaries: individuals

---

2 For an early application, see Greenbaum and Haywood (1971).

could not perform them as efficiently or as cost-effectively acting alone.[3]

For example, the collection and processing of information (e.g. on credit risk) can be more efficiently performed by intermediaries than by individual borrowers and investors and this reduces the search costs of both groups (e.g. Leland and Pyle, 1977; Campbell and Kracaw, 1980; Diamond, 1984; Ramakrishnan and Thakor, 1984; Millon and Thakor, 1985; Boyd and Prescott, 1986). The other two functions of financial intermediaries involve asset transformation. One, maturity transformation, resolves the Hicksian (1939) 'constitutional weakness' of unintermediated financial markets through intermediaries holding the long-term illiquid liabilities of deficit sectors and creating short-term liquid liabilities which the surplus sectors wish to hold as assets. As a result of this particular transformation of asset characteristics, financial intermediaries incur substantial maturity mismatches on their balance sheets which leads to various kinds of risk: price risk, inflation risk, interest rate risk, liquidity risk, exchange rate risk, basis risk[4] and default risk. The intermediary aims to reduce these risks by performing its third function, namely risk transformation through diversification, thereby creating an additional transformation of asset characteristics. The intermediaries are

3 Of course, in a perfect market with no frictions such as transactions or information costs or regulations, financial intermediaries would not exist: individuals could costlessly replicate all the activities of financial intermediaries themselves (e.g. Fama, 1980). But neither would a *process* of financial innovation exist. Under such conditions, apart from those that arise as a result of exogenous technological change, all assets would have been around since the beginning of time. Only with increasing returns to scale or with certain types of market imperfections (e.g. incomplete markets or informational asymmetries), will there be financial intermediaries and an endogenous process of financial innovation. For an alternative approach based explicitly on transaction cost economics, see Williamson (1981, 1988) who extends the seminal work of Coase (1937). For an analysis of financial innovations when markets are incomplete, see Detemple (1990).

4 The basis is the difference or spread between two interest rates or two prices, e.g. the difference between a lending rate and a borrowing rate or the difference between a futures price and a spot price. Basis risk (also known as spread risk) is the risk of an adverse movement in the basis, such as a narrowing of the spread between the lending rate and the borrowing rate.

compensated for providing these functions through intermediation spreads (i.e. by charging various liquidity and risk premia). Financial intermediaries are also involved in disintermediation activities through the provision of services that earn them fee-based income.

We can develop the characteristics model by starting with a financial institution intermediating between a typical primary borrower and a typical ultimate lender. We will assume in this section that the set of external characteristics (related to delivery systems and organisations) is given, so that financial intermediation is concerned with the transformation of the internal characteristics of assets between the end-users of the financial system. Internal characteristics refer to the characteristics of assets that do not depend on the delivery systems and organisations that provide them, e.g. expected return, risk, degree of liquidity (i.e. the time or cost to liquidate a security), term to maturity, divisibility, brokerage (issue/underwriting/transactions) costs, degree of reversibility (i.e. bid–ask spread), effect on leverage, indenture/covenant restrictions, degree of seniority, degree of voting rights, location (domestic, abroad, off-shore), balance sheet visibility and tax liability.[5]

The objective of the primary borrower (which for simplicity we take to be a firm) is to select the capital structure that maximises the value of the firm (or equivalently minimises its cost of capital). To achieve this objective, it will issue primary liabilities with

---

5 Whilst this list of characteristics is quite extensive, one of the principal aims of the characteristics model is to simplify matters by explaining behaviour in terms of as small a number of characteristics as possible. It is possible to argue that there are only two relevant characteristics: expected return and risk. For example, from the borrower's viewpoint, credit or quality rating or any change to gearing affects the cost of issue and thus the expected return. So do brokerage costs. Indenture/ covenant restrictions usually increase the borrower's risk. An appropriate maturity period lowers liquidity risk. Similarly, from the lender's viewpoint, the degree of liquidity, marketability and seniority affect his risk, and brokerage costs his return. Even in the case of balance sheet visibility and tax liability, these characteristics are only relevant when specific imperfections in the accounting and tax systems exist and, again, they will affect return and risk. Nevertheless, the fuller list of characteristics is presented in order to demonstrate the generality of the characteristics model.

a particular embodiment of characteristics. Formally, the firm performs the following exercise:[6]

$$\underset{q^s}{\text{Max}}\, v = p^{s'}q^s \quad \text{s.t.} \quad z^s = F^s(q^s) \tag{1}$$

where v is the value of the firm, q^s is the set of N^s primary liabilities comprising the firm's capital structure, p^s is the set of market prices for those liabilities, and z^s is the bundle of K internal characteristics supplied by the primary liabilities as quantified by the relationship $F^s(.)$.

The first-order conditions for a maximum of (1) with N^s liabilities and K internal characteristics are:

$$p_i^s = \sum_{j}^{K} \lambda_j^s f_{ji}^s(q^s), \quad i = 1, N^s \tag{2}$$

where λ_j^s is the shadow price of the jth characteristic supplied and $f_{ji}^s = \partial z_j^s / \partial q_i^s$ is the marginal quantity of the jth characteristic supplied by the ith liability. Now the N^s-equation system (2) implicitly provides the solution to the optimal capital structure conditional on the set of characteristics supplied.

The objective of the ultimate lender (which for simplicity we take to be a household) is to maximise a utility function defined on a set of characteristics demanded subject to a wealth constraint. To achieve this objective the household will demand ultimate assets with a particular embodiment of characteristics. Formally, the household performs the following exercise:

$$\underset{q^d}{\text{Max}}\, u = u(z^d) \quad \text{s.t.} \quad w = p^{d'}q^d \quad \text{and} \quad z^d = F^d(q^d) \tag{3}$$

where $u(.)$ is the household utility function, w is household wealth, q^d is the set of N^d ultimate assets desired by the household, p^d is the

---

6 Note that while (1) does not formally involve a wealth constraint, the firm is constrained from increasing q^s unrestrictedly and hence making v, the value of the firm, infinite. This is because the financial system is constrained by the wealth of the household sector which ultimately owns both the firm and the financial intermediary. The financial system's wealth constraint is $w = v + y$ where w is household wealth and y is the value of the financial intermediary. The financial system's wealth constraint is recognised in (5) below rather than in (1).

set of market prices for those assets, z^d is the bundle of K internal characteristics demanded, and $F^d(.)$ is a relationship that quantifies the characteristics embodied in the ultimate assets.

The first-order conditions for a maximum with N^d assets and K characteristics are:

$$p_i^d = \sum_j^K \lambda_j^d f_{ji}^d(q^d), \quad i = 1, N^d \tag{4}$$

where $\lambda_j^d = (1/\lambda^d)(\partial u / \partial z_j^d)$ is the shadow price of the jth characteristic demanded (λ^d being the marginal utility of wealth) and $f_{ji}^d = \partial z_j^d / \partial q_i^d$ is the marginal quantity of the jth characteristic contained in the ith asset. Now the N^d-equation system (4) (plus the wealth constraint) implicitly provides the solution to the optimal holdings of assets, conditional on characteristics demanded.

Intermediating between the primary borrower and the ultimate lender is the financial intermediary. The rationale for intermediation lies in the fact that, at existing prices, $z^s \neq z^d$, that is, the combination of internal characteristics embodied in primary liabilities are not those most desired by holders of ultimate assets. Whilst there might exist prices that would equate z^d with z^s even without intermediation, we assume that both household utility and firm value are lower at these prices than under a solution with intermediation.

One role of the financial intermediary is to buy-in the primary liabilities of the firm, unbundle and repackage the characteristics contained in them and issue a set of ultimate assets to households. In short, the intermediary absorbs one set of claims and produces another. This is a costly exercise and constitutes the value-added of the intermediary. The objective of the intermediary is to maximise this value-added or spread:

$$\text{Max}_{z^s} y = p^{d'} q^d - p^{s'} q^s \quad \text{s.t.} \quad q^d = F(z^s) \quad \text{and} \quad z^s = F^s(q^s) \tag{5}$$

where y is the intermediary's value-added and $F(.)$ is the intermediary's 'production function' or asset-characteristics technology that links 'inputs' (characteristics supplied by the firm's liabilities, z^s) to 'outputs' (assets demanded by households, q^d).

The first-order conditions for a maximum with K characteristics are:

$$\sum_{j}^{N^d} p_j^d f_{ji}(z^s) - \sum_{j}^{N^s} p_j^s f_{ij}^s(z^s)^{-1} = 0, \quad i = 1, K \tag{6}$$

where $f_{ji} = \partial q_j^d / \partial z_i^s$ is the change in demand for the jth asset in response to a change in the input of the ith characteristic. Now the K-equation system (6) solves for the financial intermediary's optimal holding of characteristics, z^s, as a function of p^d and p^s. Given these, the intermediary uses the asset-characteristics technology $q^d = F(z^s)$ to determine its optimal production of ultimate assets, q^d, with characteristics, z^s, conditional on prices, p^d and p^s:

$$q^d = F(z^s(p^d, p^s)). \tag{7}$$

The effect of financial intermediation is illustrated in Figure 3.1 in the case of two characteristics, z_1, (the negative of) risk, and z_2, liquidity. The intermediary buys claims with characteristics z^s, and sells claims with characteristics z^d (that is, with lower risk and greater liquidity), thereby enhancing household welfare. A natural measure of the extent or degree of financial intermediation

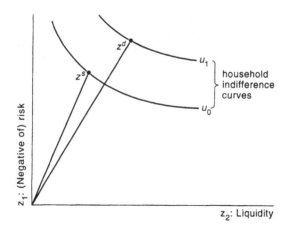

Figure 3.1 The effect of financial intermediation.

(DFI_0) is provided by the norm of the difference between z^d and z^s:

$$DFI_0 = \|z^d - z^s\|. \tag{8}$$

Financial intermediaries also engage in activities which do not involve intermediation but which generate fee-income rather than a spread. Examples are investment banks in deals that are not fully underwritten and banks engaged in foreign exchange trading and contingent liabilities such as bankers' acceptances, note-issuing facilities and revolving underwriting facilities. These activities involve partial or even complete disintermediation. For example, an investment bank might advise a firm in tailoring the terms of a bond issue to the needs of investors. In return, the bank receives a fee, generally related to the size of the deal, but does not engage in any asset transformation activity itself.

With this type of activity, the intermediary simply advises the firm to design its liabilities q^s so that z^s equals z^d. The firm is advised to perform the following exercise:

$$\underset{q^s}{\text{Max}} \, v = p^{s'} q^s \quad \text{s.t.} \quad z^d = z^s = F^s(q^s). \tag{9}$$

The first-order conditions for a maximum are:

$$p_i^s = \sum_{j}^{K} \lambda_j f_{ji}^s(q^s), \quad i = 1, N^s \tag{10}$$

where λ_j is the shadow price of the jth characteristic (supplied and demanded) and now $f_{ji}^s = \partial z_j^d / \partial q_i^s$. The N^s-equation system (10) solves for the optimal supply of the firm's liabilities conditional on the set of characteristics demanded by the household.

The financial intermediary receives a fee (y) which will typically be some proportion of γ of the size of the deal:

$$y = \gamma(p^{s'} q^s) \quad 0 < \gamma < 1. \tag{11}$$

The intermediary and the firm will bargain over the size of γ with the outcome depending on the degree of competition amongst financial intermediaries. The net value of the firm will therefore be:

$$v = (1 - \gamma)(p^{s'} q^s). \tag{12}$$

Both the financial intermediary and the firm have an incentive to maximise the value of the firm, although they will argue over the size of γ. Financial intermediaries will have an incentive to move away from intermediation towards fee-based services when y in (11) exceeds y in (5) (both net of expenses). In the case of financial intermediaries earning fee-income rather than a spread, equation (8) does not provide the appropriate measure of the degree of financial intermediation, since, if the financial intermediary is successful, equation (8) will take the value zero: there is no equivalent of (8) in terms of characteristics in this case.

3.3 The characteristics model of financial innovation

Although the basic financial services have remained essentially unchanged over time, there exists a process of financial innovation which leads to new types of assets, delivery systems and organisations. Equation (8) measures the degree of financial intermediation and also the first stage of financial innovation. But it does not describe the *process* of financial innovation.[7] For the innovation process to be evolutionary, there must be costs to the introduction of new assets, delivery systems or organisations. Over time, these costs must decline, but at any particular time, they can be substantially fixed and the marginal costs can be low.[8] Alternatively, costless opportunities to innovate could arise exogenously and slowly over time. This is on the supply side. On the demand side, there will also be factors such as changing habits (e.g. reducing

---

7 Schumpeter (1939) distinguished between invention, innovation and the diffusion of innovations. We concentrate our attention in this chapter on innovation. We have little to say about invention, which is essentially a non-economic activity. Nor do we have much to say about the diffusion of innovations, since in the case of financial innovations, competitive or rivalry pressures tend to make the diffusion process a very rapid one (see also the next footnote).

8 This is true whether the market structure for financial intermediation is perfectly competitive, imperfectly competitive or monopolistic. However, it is likely that the market structure will affect the rate of diffusion of financial innovations. Some (most notably Schumpeter, 1939) have argued that monopoly power is the main source of innovation. Others have argued that it is competition that leads to the fastest development of new products (e.g. Dasgupta and Stiglitz, 1980). Where there is imperfect competition, rivalry is regarded as the main source of innovation (e.g. Kamien and Schwartz, 1975; Scherer, 1967, 1980; Silber, 1975, 1981). Rivalry

information technology phobia or increasing risk-taking), that lead to innovation occurring as a process over time. Similarly, there are innovations in marketing which can lead to existing products being sold to new client groups, or to apparently 'new' products being marketed when they are really 'old' products suitably repackaged.

3.3.1 Supply-side innovations

To begin with in this section, we hold the set of internal characteristics fixed and consider changes to the set of external characteristics. We then consider enhancing the set of internal characteristics. To account for the process of financial innovation from the supply side, we modify the production function facing the financial intermediary as follows:

$$q_t^d = F(z^s; \theta_t) \tag{13}$$

where θ_t is a set of M external characteristics that defines (or 'constrains') the intermediary and the delivery and information-processing systems that it uses at time t. So (13) defines assets in terms of the internal characteristics that they possess, the intermediary that produces them, the delivery system through which they are marketed and the date at which they are produced. In order to capture these different effects, we will partition θ_t into $\theta_t = \{T_t, C_t, R_t\}$, which respectively represent the technology, constraints and regulations facing the intermediate at time t. This partition is consistent with existing supply-side explanations of financial innovations, especially those of Silber (1975, 1983) and Kane (1981, 1983).

---

theory predicts (see Scherer, 1980) that the pace of innovation increases with the number of evenly matched rivals, since the potential for the innovator to increase market share is greater. Dominant firms will innovate only when their market share is challenged by smaller rivals, otherwise they have little incentive to innovate in terms of enhanced market share. The conclusion of rivalry theory is that it is the competitive challenge of the rival rather than monopoly power that stimulates innovations. The same conclusion also applies to the rate of diffusion of financial innovations (e.g. Reinganum, 1981). In terms of financial innovations, it is clear that the competitive/rivalry model is the most appropriate for explaining the rate of diffusion.

With this modification the optimal production of ultimate assets q_t^d is determined by (cf. (7)):

$$q_t^d = F(z^s(p_t^d, p_t^s); \theta_t).$$ (14)

Financial innovations follow when $N_t^d > N_{t-1}^d$ so that $q_t^d = \{q_{t-1}^d, q_{kt}^d\}$ where q_{kt}^d is the new asset (or set of new assets) created during t.[9]

We can define the shadow prices of the external characteristics in terms of their effects on the financial intermediary's value added:

$$\pi_{it} = \frac{\partial y_t}{\partial \theta_{it}} = \sum_{j}^{N_t^d} p_{jt}^d \psi_{jit}, \quad i = 1, M$$ (15)

where $\psi_{jit} = \partial q_{jt}^d / \partial \theta_{it}$ is the change in demand for the jth asset if there is a marginal increase in the ith external characteristic at time t. For there to be an incentive to innovate at t, it is necessary that $\psi_{kit} > 0$ for *all* potential new assets (q_{kt}^d) and for *some* external characteristic (θ_{it}). Equivalently, the following set of inequalities must hold for *some* θ_{it}:

$$\left. \frac{dq_{jt}^d}{dq_{kt}^d} \right|_{q_{kt}^d=0}^{dy_t=0} > \left. \frac{dq_{jt}^d}{dq_{kt}^d} \right|_{q_{kt}^d=0}^{d\theta_{it}=0}, \quad \text{all } k, \text{all } j \neq k.$$ (16)

If the reverse inequality in (16) holds for all θ_{it}, then there will be a corner solution and the optimal output of q_{kt}^d will be zero (in addition $\psi_{kit} = 0$, all i). In other words, only if the 'slope' of the objective function (i.e. intermediary's value-added) (evaluated in (q_{jt}^d, q_{kt}^d) space at $q_{kt}^d = 0$) exceeds the 'slope' of at least one 'constraint' will there be an incentive to innovate and hence a movement from a corner solution to an interior equilibrium.

While $\psi_{kit} > 0$ and (16) are necessary conditions for an innovation to occur, they are not sufficient. This can be seen by looking more closely at the components of θ_t.

---

9 We are associating financial innovations with increases in the number of ultimate assets demanded. It is, of course, possible for financial innovations to be associated with increases in primary liabilities supplied (i.e. $N_t^s > N_{t-1}^s$).

Technology-induced innovations

The first component of θ_t is T_t, the set of characteristics defining the technology (e.g. delivery or information-processing systems) available to financial intermediaries. Suppose that before t, the non-availability of a particular technology constituted a binding constraint on the introduction of a new asset, $\psi_{kT,t-1} > 0$ and $q^d_{k,t-1} = 0$. There is an incentive to innovate but no means of doing so. The innovation will not occur until the technology is available at t. If the innovation is introduced in period t, it occurs either exogenously if the new technology is introduced spontaneously, or endogenously if the new technology is developed in response to the lost profit opportunities (i.e. a high shadow price $\psi_{kT,t-1}$) observed in the previous period. Many of the technological improvements in the money transmission system can be explained in this way.

Constraint-induced innovations

The second component of θ_t is C_t, the set of characteristics defining the constraints (either internally (i.e. prudentially) or externally imposed) facing the intermediary. In this case, the incentive to innovate is given by $\psi_{kCt} > \psi^*_{kC} > \psi_{kC,t-1}$. This implies that the cost of abiding by a constraint has been increasing over time and has passed some threshold (ψ^*_{kC}) above which the cost of the constraint in terms of lost profit opportunities has become excessive. Constraint-induced innovations are distinct from technology-induced innovations: in the former case, the constraints can be avoided (either by changing the mix of claims or the delivery system for marketing the claims or the organisational form of the financial institution), but in the latter case the absence of appropriate technology is unavoidable.

Regulation-induced innovations

The final component of θ_t is R_t, the set of characteristics specifying the regulations or the regulatory reaction functions facing the intermediary. Here the problem is more complex than with technology or with constraints because of the reactive nature of regulations, involving a noncooperative dynamic game played between the regulators and the regulated intermediary. Each player's optimal strategy depends on the strategy that the other player is expected to pursue (not only in the current period but in all future periods that the game is played) but does not involve any cooperation with the other player. In the Nash version of the game, each player assumes that the other will attempt to counteract its own action. In the Stackelberg version, the leader moves first and the follower reacts passively.

In deciding its innovation strategy, the financial intermediary must take into account the regulatory authority's objective function. We could motivate this objective function as follows. The regulatory authority wishes to encourage financial innovations and competition between financial intermediaries but has a responsibility for prudential regulation, so is concerned not to allow excess credit or excess risk, with their attendant inflationary and bankruptcy consequences, to build up in the economy. Historically, the evidence suggests that financial intermediaries have acted as Stackelberg leaders in developing new financial products and the regulatory authorities have behaved like Stackelberg followers, reacting with a lag to the developments in the financial world. But recently, the authorities have been trying to predict what the intermediaries will do in future and take this into account when they revise their regulations. Examples of this have been the 1980 Deposit Institution Deregulation and Monetary Control Act in the US, and the 1980/1987 Banking Acts and 1986 Building Societies Act in the UK.

Using this framework, we can interpret (14) not so much as an optimal decision rule, but as a policy reaction function. A similar reaction function exists for the regulatory authority. For example, the solution in the Nash game (i.e. the subgame-perfect Nash equilibrium (see, e.g., Selten, 1965; Kreps and Wilson, 1982)) requires that both reaction functions are optimised across both players and over all time periods simultaneously. Because of this simultaneity, the optimal strategies will be determined implicitly rather than analytically as in (14). The solution will be of the form $\tilde{q}^d = \{q_1^d(\tilde{R}), ..., q_\infty^d(\tilde{R})\}$, i.e. the set of the intermediary's optimal planned strategies (namely, the production of claims from $t = 1, \infty$), and $\tilde{R} = \{R_1(\tilde{q}^d), ..., R_\infty(\tilde{q}^d)\}$, i.e. the set of the regulatory authority's optimal anticipated strategies (namely, the regulations in force from $t = 1, \infty$).

Again, it is possible to explain the process generating new assets in terms of the costs of adhering to the regulations in force. The costs are given by the shadow prices (ψ_{kRt}) in (15). When these shadow prices grow over time and exceed the threshold, there is a strong incentive to innovate either by existing institutions or by new institutions established to bypass the existing regulations; and the design of the innovation will anticipate the response of the regulator in current and future periods. Consequently, it is important to differentiate assets according to the institutions that issue them. So, for example, an asset from a regulated deposit-taking institution is different from an asset from an unregulated deposit-taking institution, even though they may have identical internal characteristics. This is because the unregulated institution can alter more easily the characteristics mix of its assets, equivalent to a further innovation, than can the regulated institution in response to changes in regulations by the regulatory authority. However, this does not imply that the regulated institution is in a completely disadvantaged position because it too is able, to a certain extent, to alter the characteristics mix of its assets in a way that substitutes away from the effects of the new regulations. Furthermore, regulations can sometimes work in favour of the regulated intermediary. For example, in the case of deposit insurance and US thrifts, regulation, by enhancing confidence, tends to increase the stock market value of the intermediary in the short run.

3.3.2 *Demand-side innovations*

To account for the process of financial innovation on the demand side, we return to equation (4) which provides the implicit demand for assets, given wealth, prices, characteristics, etc.

An intermediary introduces a new asset q_k^d with a new combination of internal characteristics. For example, in line with the Cross Report's characterisation of innovations, it could be (price or credit) risk-transferring, liquidity-enhancing, credit-generating or equity-generating. There will be a new asset-characteristics technology $z^d = F(q^d, q_k^d)$ and a new wealth constraint $w = p^{d'}q^d + p_k^q q_k^d$. The resulting demand for the $N^d + 1$ assets is determined by:

$$p_i^d = \sum_j^K \lambda_j^d f_{ji}^d(q^d, q_k^d) \quad i = 1, N^d + 1. \tag{17}$$

This system of $(N^d + 1)$ equations will in general provide different optimal holdings for q^d compared with (4) because of the new asset-characteristics technology facing investors, $f_{ji}^d(q^d, q_k^d)$, and because of the substitution effects that are induced by the innovation. If we assume that all assets are gross substitutes, then the lower is p_k^d, the issue price of q_k^d, the higher will be the demand for the new asset and the lower will be the demand for existing assets.

In (17), we kept $\lambda_j^d = \lambda_j^d(w)$, the preferences for characteristics, constant. But an important source of demand for financial innovations is likely to be increases in wealth (see, e.g., Gurley and Shaw, 1955, 1956). Wealth-induced innovations will arise when increases in wealth reduce the shadow prices λ_j^d of demanding characteristics. Similarly, changes in tastes, also reflected in changes in λ_j^d, could lead to the introduction of new assets, delivery systems or organisations. For example, increasing computer literacy has helped the introduction and spread of computer-related financial services such as home banking and share shops.

3.3.3   New internal characteristics

It is also possible for new internal characteristics to be introduced, both on the supply side (i.e. z^s) and on the demand side (i.e. z^d). Changes in z^s lead to a new set of inputs into the intermediary's production function, while changes in z^d lead to a new asset-characteristics technology. It is clear that financial innovations could be induced by such changes.

In practice, it is rare for completely new characteristics to be discovered since, as Niehans (1983) argues, most 'new' characteristics can usually be constructed as a combination of existing ones. However, an extremely important recent example is provided by the introduction of financial options and related derivatives. The most important characteristic of an option is that its expiry price distribution is concentrated on one side of the exercise price. It is not possible (in practice) to replicate this characteristic with any other asset or combination of assets.[10] But its existence now permits hedging strategies that were simply not feasible in the past.

Finally we note that a natural measure of the degree of financial innovation in period t is given by (cf. (8)):

$$DFI_t = \|(z_t^d - z_{t-1}^d) - (z_t^s - z_{t-1}^s)\|. \tag{18}$$

---

10   It is, of course, possible in theory to replicate the price behaviour of an option by switching continuously between Treasury bills and the underlying security. In practice, however, the costs of doing this would be prohibitive.

In terms of external characteristics, the degree of financial innovation will equal $\|\theta_t - \theta_{t-1}\|$.

Financial innovations have occurred in a particular historical sequence and they also appear to have occurred in definite waves rather than randomly. These phenomena can also be explained in terms of the characteristics framework developed here.

The sequence of innovations can be explained if the rising shadow prices (15) of abiding by existing technology, constraints and regulations pass their thresholds at different times. The sequence of innovations should correspond to the sequence in which these thresholds were triggered. For example, Ben-Horim and Silber (1977), using data on the First National City Bank for the period 1952–72, found that increases in deposit and capital shadow prices coincided with the introduction of certificates of deposit (in 1961), subordinated debentures (between 1963 and 1965), eurodollars (in 1969) and bank-related commercial paper and loan repurchase (in 1969).

It is also clear how the sequence of innovations can be bunched together over time. When the shadow price thresholds are triggered, a whole range of new assets with a very similar mix of characteristics will be created at about the same time. While all the innovations are in response to the same threshold being reached (and are therefore essentially identical), they are likely to be produced by competing financial intermediaries. Examples here are: the various types of credit cards; electronic funds transfer systems at the point of sale (EFT/POS); innovations in bond markets such as the different types of coupon-stripped instruments introduced by Salomon Bros (CATS), Lehman Bros (LIONS), Merrill Lynch (TIGRS) and the US Treasury itself on US Treasury bonds (STRIPS) (see also Mason, 1986; Levich, 1988; Matthews, 1994, Table 2-1); and asset securitisation, particularly in banking (see Greenbaum, 1987).[11]

Other explanations for innovation waves are the business cycle or the political cycle. If causal factors such as wealth (or income)

---

11 Even if it could be argued that much of the proliferation in identical new products from competing institutions is the result of nonprice competition and the need to preserve market share in the face of first-mover advantage (see, e.g., Anderson and Harris, 1986; Tufano, 1989), it is also possible to explain the ability of such institutions to introduce these products at about the same time in terms of some characteristic shadow price threshold being triggered.

fluctuate with the business cycle, then we should expect financial innovations to broadly follow the pattern of the business cycle.[12] Changes in governments could also lead to rapid innovation, if the change in government is also associated with a change in regulatory regime.

3.4 Conclusion

The opportunity for empirical work on financial intermediation and financial innovations using the characteristics model is substantial. Equations (2), (4), (6), (10), (15) and (17) have the form of (non-linear-in-variables) regression equations. They therefore provide the basis for an empirical test of the validity of the characteristics model, both in time-series and in cross-section form. Assuming that data on variables such as f_{ji}, f_{ji}^s and f_{ji}^d can be collected, testing the importance of the jth characteristic reduces to a test of the significance of the 'regression coefficients' λ_j^d and λ_j^s.

In addition, statistically significant peaks in the time paths of the shadow prices given in (15) should correspond with periods of rapid financial innovation. Prior to an innovation, we would expect to find a statistically insignificant value for the shadow price associated with a particular external characteristic (π_{it}), suggesting that there is no incentive to innovate. Then gradually, the shadow price begins to rise as the cost of not introducing available technology or the cost of abiding by a constraint or a regulation begins to grow. Once this cost has become excessive, an innovation or a series of innovations that use the new technology or that avoid the constraint or regulation will occur. After this stage, the shadow prices decline rapidly to zero again. This is on the supply side. On the demand side, tests will be based on (17). A new asset will only be successful if it contains a significant amount of a desirable characteristic or a significant reduction in an undesirable characteristic relative to existing assets, so that f_{ji}^d is significantly different from zero for *some j*. Testing the significance of the model as a whole reduces to testing whether the degree of financial intermediation given by (8) or the degree of financial innovation given by (18) is significantly different from zero.

12 Schumpeter (1939) argues that it is the bunching together of innovations that causes the business cycle.

Finally, the characteristics model has a potentially powerful contribution to make in the important new field of security design (see Allen and Gale, 1989, 1994; Harris and Raviv, 1989; Boot and Thakor, 1993; Nachman and Noe, 1994; Duffie and Rahi, 1995).

References

Allen, F. and Gale, D. (1989). Optimal security design. *Review of Financial Studies*, 1, 229–63.

Allen, F. and Gale, D. (1994). *Financial Innovation and Risk Sharing*. Cambridge, Mass.: MIT Press.

Anderson, R. W. and Harris, C. J. (1986). A model of innovation with application to new financial products. *Oxford Economic Papers* (Supplement), 38, 203–18.

Ben-Horim, M. and Silber, W. L. (1977). Financial innovation—a linear programming approach. *Journal of Banking and Finance*, 1, 277–96.

Benston, G. J. and Smith, C. W. (1976). A transactions cost approach to the theory of financial intermediation. *Journal of Finance*, 31, 215–31.

Boot, A. W. A. and Thakor, A. V. (1993). Security design. *Journal of Finance*, 48, 1349–78.

Boyd, J. H. and Prescott, E. C. (1986). Financial intermediary coalitions. *Journal of Economic Theory*, 38, 211–32.

Campbell, T. S. and Kracaw, W. A. (1980). Information production, market signalling, and the theory of financial intermediation. *Journal of Finance*, 35, 863–82.

Coase, R. H. (1937). The nature of the firm. *Economica*, 4, 386–405.

Cross, S. Y. (Chairman) (1986). *Recent Innovations in International Banking*. Basle, Switzerland: Bank for International Settlements.

Dasgupta, P. and Stiglitz, J. (1980). Uncertainty, industrial structure and the speed of R & D. *Bell Journal of Economics*, 11, 1–28.

Detemple, J. B. (1990). Financial innovation, values and volatilities when markets are incomplete. *Geneva Papers on Risk and Insurance*, 15, 47–54.

Diamond, D. W. (1984). Financial intermediation and delegated monitoring. *Review of Economic Studies*, 51, 393–414.

Duffie, D. and Rahi, R. (1995). Financial market innovation and security design. *Journal of Economic Theory*, 65, 1–42.

Fama, E. F. (1980). Banking in the theory of finance. *Journal of Monetary Economics*, 6, 39–58.

Greenbaum, S. I. (ed) (1987). Asset securitisation and off-balance sheet risks of depository institutions. *Journal of Banking and Finance*, 11, 355–548.

Greenbaum, S. I. and Haywood, C. F. (1971). Secular changes in the financial services industry. *Journal of Money, Credit and Banking*, 3, 571–89.

Greenbaum, S. I. and Higgins, B. (1983). Financial innovation. In Benston, G. J. (ed) *Financial Services: The Changing Institutions and Government Policy.* Englewood Cliffs, NJ: Prentice-Hall.

Gurley, J. G. and Shaw, E. S. (1955). Financial aspects of economic development. *American Economic Review*, 45, 515–38.

Gurley, J. G. and Shaw, E. S. (1956). Financial intermediaries and the saving-investment process. *Journal of Finance*, 11, 257–76.

Harris, M. and Raviv, A. (1989). The design of securities. *Journal of Financial Economics*, 24, 255–87.

Hicks, J. R. (1939). *Value and Capital.* Oxford: Oxford University Press.

Kamien, M. and Schwartz, N. (1975). Market structure and innovative activity: A survey. *Journal of Economic Literature*, 13, 1–37.

Kane, E. J. (1981). Accelerating inflation, technological innovation and the decreasing effectiveness of banking regulation. *Journal of Finance*, 36, 355–67.

Kane, E. J. (1983). Policy implications of structure changes in financial markets. *American Economic Review*, 73, 96–100.

Kreps, D. M. and Wilson, R. (1982). Sequential equilibrium. *Econometrica*, 50, 863–94.

Leland, H. E. and Pyle, D. H. (1977). Informational asymmetries, financial structure, and financial intermediation. *Journal of Finance*, 32, 371–87.

Levich, R. M. (1988). Financial innovations in international financial markets. In Feldstein, M. (ed) *The United States and the World Economy.* Chicago: University of Chicago Press.

Mason, R. (1986). *Innovations in the Structures of International Securities.* London: Credit Suisse First Boston.

Matthews, J. (1994). *Struggle and Survival on Wall Street: The Economics of Competition Among Securities Firms.* New York: Oxford University Press.

Miller, M. H. (1986). Financial innovation: The last twenty years and the next. *Journal of Financial and Quantitative Analysis*, 21, 459–71.

Miller, M. H. (1991). *Financial Innovations and Market Volatility.* Oxford: Basil Blackwell.

Millon, M. H. and Thakor, A. V. (1985). Moral hazard and information sharing: A model of financial information gathering agencies. *Journal of Finance*, 40, 1403–22.

Nachman, D. and Noe, T. (1994). Optimal design of securities under asymmetric information. *Review of Financial Studies*, 7, 1–44.

Niehans, J. (1983). Financial innovation, multinational banking, and monetary policy. *Journal of Banking and Finance*, 7, 537–51.

Ramakrishnan, R. T. S. and Thakor, A. V. (1984). Information reliability and a theory of financial intermediation. *Review of Economic Studies*, 51, 415–32.

Reinganum, J. (1981). Market structure and the diffusion of new technology. *Bell Journal of Economics*, 12, 618–24.

Ross, S. A. (1989). Institutional markets, financial marketing, and financial innovation. *Journal of Finance*, 64, 541–56.

Scherer, F. M. (1967). Research and development resource allocation under rivalry. *Quarterly Journal of Economics*, 81, 359–94.

Scherer, F. M. (1980). *Industrial Market Structure and Economic Performance*. Chicago: Rand McNally.

Schumpeter, J. A. (1939). *Business Cycles*. New York: McGraw-Hill.

Selten, R. (1965). Spieltheoretische Behandlung eines Oligopolmodells mit Nachfragetragheit. *Zeitschrift für Gesamte Stattswissenschaft*, 121, 301–24.

Silber, W. L. (1975). *Financial Innovations*. Lexington, Mass.: D.C. Heath.

Silber, W. L. (1981). Innovation, competition and new contract design in futures markets. *Journal of Futures Markets*, 1, 123–55.

Silber, W. L. (1983). The process of financial innovation. *American Economic Review*, 73, 89–95.

Tufano, P. (1989). Financial innovation and first-mover advantage. *Journal of Financial Economics*, 25, 213–40.

Williamson, O. E. (1981). The economics of organisation: The transaction cost approach. *American Journal of Sociology*, 87, 548–77.

Williamson, O. E. (1988). Transaction cost economics. In Schmalensee, R. and Willig, R. (eds) *Handbook of Industrial Organisation*. Amsterdam: North-Holland.

Chapter 4

A characteristics definition of financial markets

Shelagh A. Heffernan

The characteristics model is used here to define and classify financial products and markets. Based on recent changes in the United Kingdom, the model is used to illustrate how applied economists might analyse the impact of regulatory and technological changes on financial markets.

4.1 Introduction

This chapter develops a concept of financial markets that will encompass all financial products offered in such markets, independent of the specifics of national markets or products offered by segments of a somewhat loosely defined 'aggregate' financial market. Section 4.2 uses the characteristics approach to develop definitions of a financial product and a financial market. Section 4.3 demonstrates how these definitions can be used to explore the impact of regulatory and technological changes on the demand side of financial markets. Reforms of the UK stock market are briefly considered to demonstrate how the model might be used to analyse the effects of regulatory and technological change. Section 4.4 briefly considers the supply side, though most of the chapter is devoted to a specification of the demand side because this is where the greatest gaps in the literature occur. Section 4.5 concludes and explores avenues for further research.

Reprinted from *Journal of Banking and Finance*, Vol. 14, pp. 583–609, © 1990, with permission from Elsevier Science, Oxford.

4.2   Financial products and financial markets: definitions

According to the characteristics model, the utility of an individual or household is dependent on the characteristics that make up the goods and services consumed by that individual or household. We will assume that households, as buyers of financial products, expect to obtain three characteristics from the purchase of financial goods. These are the expected rate of return $E(R)$, security, and liquidity.

The expected rate of return is the mean yield on an asset plus the forecast gain (loss) net of transactions costs.

The security of an asset is captured by a parameter reflecting the spread of returns that can materialise in different states of the world, i.e. it is the difference between maximum and minimum returns. The narrower the spread, *ceteris paribus*, the greater the security of the asset. It is a concept of risk that differs from the better known variance of returns, the sum of the squared deviations of actual from mean returns, weighted by the probability of each return occurring. If constant absolute risk aversion and normally distributed rates of return are assumed, it is possible to employ a more traditional concept of risk, such as the variance or the standard deviation of returns. Spread was chosen because it is analytically simpler and will ease the task of obtaining a measure for risk when this model is used in applied work.[1] Precedents for the use of spread as a measure of risk include Stiglitz and Weiss (1981, 1983). In studies of credit rationing and incentive effects, these authors assume that the borrower has control over the mean-preserving spread on the project for which funding is being applied, which the lender cannot observe.

Liquidity is the absence of illiquidity, defined as the cost of conversion into an acceptable medium of exchange on immediate notice, or with no more than an accepted and specified period of delay. If an asset is perfectly liquid, there is no time or cost associated with the agent transacting or holding the asset.

Liquidity is often treated as one of several types of risk associated with financial transactions. Others include market, credit, currency, settlement, and sovereign risks. For example, market liquidity risk is the risk that a negotiable financial instrument cannot be sold

---

1 The specific utility function chosen for much of this chapter allows direct translation from spread to variance if the return on a risky asset is normally distributed.

quickly at close to full market value. If one employs an optimal portfolio model of investment, all risks should be discounted in the expected rate of return. Why then has liquidity been singled out as one of three characteristics of financial products? The answer relates to the importance of time as a component of liquidity and the need to treat this aspect of liquidity as a separate component in the characteristics model. If an agent holds a financial product with a high proportion of the liquidity characteristic, he knows that at some point in time the financial asset may be converted rapidly and inexpensively into an acceptable medium of exchange. For example, suppose an agent opts to hold 100% of his portfolio in the notes and coins of the national government. This is a financial product with 100% of the liquidity characteristic and it ensures that the agent will hold a means of exchange (of a certain value) at any point in time. There are risks associated with 100% liquidity: inflation and the possibility that the government may default on its notes and coins. But these risks, like credit and currency risk, will be discounted in the expected return. Liquidity is singled out as a separate characteristic to isolate the importance of the time/cost in transacting an asset.

In this framework, there are two categories of financial product. A financial good or service is defined as any product that:

1   offers at least one or a combination of the three characteristics (category A product) and/or
2   enables agents to alter the characteristics combination of the portfolio currently held (category B product).

For example, the medium of exchange is a financial service offering 100% liquidity for those who hold the currency in their pockets. On the other hand, a bond with a maturity of 20 years will yield some rate of return (depending on the risk) but little in the way of liquidity, unless it is actively traded on a secondary market. Between these extremes lies a range of financial goods and services offering different combinations of the three characteristics. In addition, there are products that are *tools* by which the agent can change the combination of characteristics offered to him. An example is the use of a forward contract to hedge against currency risk.

Some of these ideas may be illustrated on a three-dimensional diagram. For simplification, assume that there is no inflation and the probability of government default is zero. Figure 4.1 illustrates

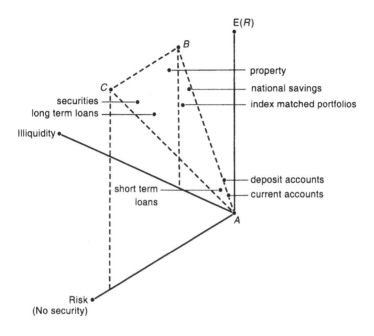

A   Cash: perfect liquidity, zero risk, zero return
B   Product with high return, high illiquidity, perfect security
C   Product with low security, high return, perfect liquidity

Figure 4.1 Characteristics frontier for category A financial products.

a typical characteristics frontier for category A financial products. It is three-dimensional, with one dimension for each characteristic. The triangle *ABC* represents the 'efficiency frontier', the efficient combinations of feasible characteristics or the maximum return for given illiquidity and security. To obtain a linear plane, assets must be perfectly divisible and the measure of illiquidity must be proportional to the amount of the asset, implying that the portfolio time management function must be quadratic in the quantity of assets. Then, the measure of illiquidity (the first derivative of the portfolio time management function with respect to a given asset) is a linear function of the asset in question.

Line *AB* is the combination of the return and illiquidity characteristics for perfect security; line *BC* is the combination of the security and liquidity characteristics for maximum return; and line AC is the combination of the return and security characteristics for zero illiquidity.

Point A represents cash: perfect liquidity, perfect security and zero return. At point B is a product that offers high illiquidity, high $E(R)$, and perfect security, and point C represents a product with perfect liquidity, low security, and high expected return. Products tend to cluster near one of the three points, making them either *liquidity-dominated* (near point A), *return-dominated* (near point C), or, less frequently, *risk-dominated* (near point B).

If one considers products currently offered by British financial institutions, there are none that can be placed at points B or C. National Savings offer high security, complete short-term illiquidity and some return and therefore are placed on line AB but closer to point B than A. Current accounts offer high liquidity, high security and low expected return and appear on line AB but very close to point A. Deposit accounts may be placed along AB just above current accounts, since they offer a higher return but are more illiquid than current accounts. Securities are more liquid than property but are less secure because they experience a relatively wide range of returns. Acknowledging the existence of primary and secondary markets for securities, securities traded in the secondary market would be more liquid and, therefore, would be placed closer to point C. If transactions costs associated with dealing in securities were to fall to zero, then they could be placed at or very close to C.

Products that appear on the assets side of the financial firm's balance sheet can be placed on the same diagram. Consider long- and short-term loans. The customer uses a financial institution to facilitate the arrangement of a debt in order to obtain an asset with some combination of the three characteristics, taking out a loan from a financial institution for one or two reasons. The loan enhances his liquidity position (short term) and/or increases the future value of an asset, such as property or a business. Short-term loans appear close to point A but near line AC, indicating high liquidity, some security and low return. Long-term loans appear closer to the centre of the efficiency plane, indicating relatively lower security (i.e. a large distance between the minimum and maximum return on the asset which the loan is used to purchase), higher expected return and lower liquidity.

Figure 4.2, a more detailed version of Figure 4.1, is used to illustrate how one represents a particular point on the *efficiency plane*.

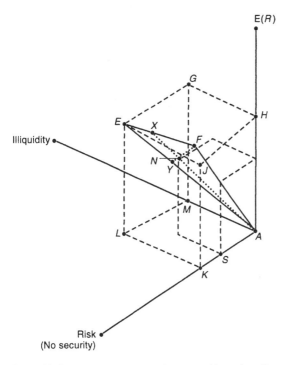

Figure 4.2 Representing a particular point, *N*, on the efficiency plane.

Suppose there are three financial products: money, deposits, and bonds. The characteristics of these three products are assumed to be such that point *F* represents a portfolio of 100% deposits, and points *A* and *E* represent portfolios of 100% cash and bonds, respectively. Points *AEF* represent a feasible efficiency plane, a subset of frontier *ABC* in Figure 4.1, that is, the combinations of characteristics available given the products offered by financial firms. The three-dimensional *financial products box* gives all the feasible combinations of characteristics for the efficiency plane *AEF*. To represent a particular point on the efficiency plane, the proportions of each characteristic in a given financial product must be known. Consider point *N*. The nearer *N* is to *E*, the more bonds are held in the portfolio, while the nearer *N* is to *F*, the more deposits are held. If *N* is close to *A*, nearly all of the portfolio is held in cash. The ratio NX/AX is the proportion of the portfolio held in cash. The proportion held in deposits is NY/FY.

A list of category A financial products is found in Table 4.1, classified as either return-, liquidity- or risk-dominated financial products. Insurance and venture capital are the only products that appear under the heading of 'risk-dominated'. Insurance offers the customer a means of insuring against some risk. Some policies are relatively easy to liquidate, others carry a high expected return. The venture capitalist is highly exposed to risk. Venture capital is a relatively illiquid form of investment but it is associated with a high expected return.

Category B financial products are also listed in Table 4.1. These 'portfolio management' products are a form of insurance against unpredictable income. Use of these products should reduce

Table 4.1 Classification of financial products in the characteristics model

Category A. Liquidity-, return- and risk-dominated financial products

Liquidity-dominated financial products
Foreign exchange facilities (except in cases of speculation)
Retail banking: deposit accounts, credit card products, current accounts,
    cash-dispensing facilities
Wholesale banking: current accounts
Short-term loans

Return-dominated financial products
Equities
Bonds
Treasury and commercial bills
Commercial paper
Unit trusts, investment trusts and open-ended investment companies
Property
Commodities
Bullion
Long-term loans
Mortgages

Risk-dominated financial products
Insurance
Venture capital

Category B. Portfolio management products

Options
Swaps
Forward and futures contracts
Underwriting
Mergers and acquisitions
Treasury management packages
Retail asset management packages

volatility of investment income and/or the costs associated with certain financial transactions.

To summarise, if the characteristics of security, expected return and liquidity are identified as the key components of a financial product, there are just two categories of financial product. In category A are financial products that contain one or more of these characteristics, and category B consists of devices that enable an agent to change the combination of characteristics available in existing financial products. A financial market involves the exchange of products that fall into one of these two categories and the financial sector is made up of firms offering one or more of these products.

The concept of a financial market put forward here is similar to the ideas implicit in Arrow's (1964) classic paper on the role of securities in the optimal allocation of risk bearing. In Arrow's complete financial market, agents may alter their exposure to all possible contingencies. In the characteristics model, an important feature of a complete market is the ability of agents to hold financial products with any desired combination of characteristics. However, while Arrow treated risk as a multidimensional concept, the advantage of the characteristics model is that it employs a relatively simple measure of risk and this renders the model more operationally relevant.

4.3 Regulatory and technological changes: the demand side

In this section, household demand is modelled to demonstrate how the characteristics approach to financial products and markets may be used to analyse the impact of changes in these markets. The framework is then used to assess the impact of British regulatory changes, with special emphasis on the reforms of the stock market. The behaviour of a firm as buyer of financial products is also discussed.

4.3.1 *Household behaviour in response to technological and regulatory changes*

In Section 4.2, the three characteristics of a financial asset were identified as expected return, security, and liquidity. In this section, the number of financial assets is limited to three:

M money,
D deposits with one type of financial institution,
B another type of financial claim.

The amount of the liquidity characteristic contained in each asset differs. The household devotes a time interval to managing financial transactions. The time interval is specified to be a function t, which varies negatively with the amount of M held and positively with holdings of B. Asset D is intermediate in terms of liquidity: holdings of D reduce t by less than M or raise t by less than B.

The expected return on M is constrained to be zero, that on D is r, and that on B is q; r is uniquely given and q is random. Thus M and D are fully secure assets in the absence of inflation risk while B is not.

The portfolio optimisation problem for the household is to allocate given wealth W between three assets, M, D and B. It is part of a more general optimisation exercise which embraces the labour supply decision, h, and consumption decision, c. To simplify matters, the analysis is confined to dealing with optimisation in a single period. Multiperiod optimisation would involve an enormous increase in complexity and is not necessary given the objective of this chapter: to demonstrate that the characteristics model is sufficiently general to allow the derivation of essential features of asset demand functions and to permit an analysis of the impact of technological and regulatory changes on household behaviour.

We will suppose that the household is endowed with wealth W and a unit of time. The conversion of wage income to consumption is treated as a financial transaction. Time may be devoted to leisure, assumed to be utility generating, or to financial transactions, t, or sold in the market place, h, for a wage of w. It is assumed that the portfolio allocations and labour supply choice are uniquely determined. The income flow that stems from these choices is stochastic, unless holdings of B are zero, by virtue of the randomness of q. This income flow is assumed to be applied in full to consumption. Consumption will therefore also be random. It is assumed that the probability density function for q is known and equal to $f(q)$.

Consumption will equal:

$$c = wh + rD + qB$$

and the household is taken to have a utility function $u(c, 1 - h - t)$. The household is assumed to be a von Neumann–Morgenstern expected utility maximiser. The problem can be presented as:

Max $E[u(c, 1 - h - t)]$,   subject to

$$c - wh - rD - qB = 0$$

$$W - M - D - B = 0$$

$$t - t(M, D, B) = 0$$

$$h \geq 0$$

$$M \geq 0$$

$$D \geq 0$$

$$B \geq 0.$$

The partial derivatives of t with respect to M, D and B are denoted t_1, t_2 and t_3.

If the non-negativity constraints are assumed not to bind at zero and u is assumed to be additively separable (i.e. $u = v[c] + z[1 - h - t]$), the optimisation problem reduces to:

$$\underset{h, D, B}{\text{Max}} \int_{-\infty}^{+\infty} f(q)v[wh + rD + qB]dq$$

$$+ z[1 - h - t(W - D - B, D, B)]. \tag{1}$$

The first-order conditions yield labour supply and asset demand functions of the form:

$$h^* = h^*(w, W, r, Eq; a; p)$$

$$M^* = M^*(w, W, r, Eq; a; p)$$

$$B^* = B^*(w, W, r, Eq; a; p)$$

$$D^* = D^*(w, W, r, Eq; a; p)$$

where a is a parameter reflecting the mean preserving spread of q, and p is a coefficient reflecting some function of $-v''/v'$ (the coefficient of absolute consumption risk aversion). Conventional qualitative priors on the first derivatives of the above functions are found in Appendix 1 to this chapter.

To illustrate, assume that parameter p is a constant, so that v can be integrated into the negative exponential form: $v(\cdot) = -e^{-p(wh+rD+qB)}$, and $f(q)$ is specialised to the uniform distribution:

$$\bar{q} + a/2 > q > \bar{q} - a/2 \quad (\Rightarrow Eq = \bar{q}) \tag{2}$$

so q has equal probabilities of taking any values within this interval.

Under these conditions, the first-order conditions for an optimum with respect to the choice variables h, D and B imply:

$$
\begin{aligned}
Bv' &= -w(e^{-pK} - e^{-pL}) \\
&= [-Z/(t_2 - t_1)](e^{-pK} - e^{-pL}) \\
&= Z/(t_3 - t_1) \\
Z &= e^{-pK} - e^{-pL} + (q + a/2)e^{-pK} - (q - a/2)e^{-pL} \\
K &= wh + rD + B(q - a/2) \\
L &= K - aB.
\end{aligned}
$$

These conditions furnish implicit asset demand functions for D and B, and also for M ($M^* = W - D^* - B^*$) and they also yield an implicit labour supply function, h^*. The optimal level of consumption, which will be state dependent, is

$$c^* = wh^* + rD^* + qB^*.$$

Suppose the time transaction function t is assumed to be additively separable:

$$t = -A_1 X_M(M) + A_2 X_D(D) + A_3 X_B(B). \tag{3}$$

Here t is the management time devoted to transactions and the X_j are the 'time cost' functions for the assets. If $A_1 > 0$, then, given $X_M' > 0$, a higher M implies a lower time cost, *ceteris paribus*. If either A_2 or A_3 is positive, then more management time is required for a higher D or B, given X_D' and $X_B' > 0$. We assume $X_M', X_D', X_B' > 0 > X_M''$ and $X_D'', X_B'' > 0$. Strictly speaking, t should also vary with consumption in (3); this is omitted in the interests of simplicity.

The illiquidity of an asset is defined by the change in time required for its portfolio management in response to a unit increase in the asset. For example, when M rises by one unit, portfolio management time declines by t_1, which means that the degree of illiquidity of the portfolio is reduced, whereas when B rises by one unit, t rises by t_3, which implies that B has illiquidity t_3.

Technical progress is defined as any new technology that allows the household to save management time in the handling of its asset portfolio.[2] Technical progress can be registered, in the case of M, by a rise in the parameter A_1: one unit of M will now save more management time than before. For $dA_1 > 0$, technical progress lowers the relative price of the liquidity characteristic of money but at the same time it will mean that less cash is needed to achieve the same level of liquidity that was in place prior to the technical progress. If there is technical progress in the transactions time for assets B or D, so that holding one unit of B or D now requires less management time, it will be reflected by a fall in the parameters A_3 and A_2, respectively.

In the context of this model, the question to be addressed is: what are the key parameters that influence the composition of the household financial portfolio? Optimisation exercises with respect to M, D and B allow us to explore how changes in key parameters (such as the yields on D, B or technical progress that saves transactions time) affect the demand for money, deposits and other financial claims. Algebraic details of these exercises are found in Appendix 2 of this chapter. Table 4.2 illustrates how a change in a given parameter affects the demand for a given asset.

With reference to Appendix 2, the second-order conditions imply that c_3, the coefficient on dB, is positive. Those on a and P (c_2 and c_1, respectively) are both negative in the neighbourhood of an optimum, establishing that an increase in the coefficient of risk aversion, or the spread parameter on B, lowers the demand for that asset. A rise in the mean expected yield on B raises the demand for B, as will technical progress that economises on the management time devoted to B, which will be reflected in a lower value of A_3. Conditions on t imply that $c_4 c_5$ should be negative: this tells us that a higher yield on asset D, or technical progress in transactions time devoted to D, should reduce the demand for B. The demand for B will rise with wealth, given that $X_M'' < 0$, and fall with technical progress, enhancing the time-saving properties of money.

---

2 We assume the new technology is in place. The process of financial innovation, whereby new technologies are introduced, is discussed in Chapter 3 and in Silber (1975, 1983) and Kane (1981, 1983).

Table 4.2 The effects of parameter changes on B, D, M

Parameters	B	D	M
q	+	−	−
r	−	+	−
a	−	+	+
W	+	+	+
A_1	−	−	+
A_2	−	+	−
A_3	+	−	−

Definition of parameters:
q: yield on B.
r: yield on D.
a: mean-preserving spread on B.
W: household wealth.
A_1: technical progress in transactions time for M ($dA_1 > 0$).
A_2: technical progress in transactions time for D ($dA_2 > 0$).
A_3: technical progress in transactions time for B ($dA_3 > 0$).

Turning to the demand for D, notice first that our assumptions on t imply that $c_6 > 0$ and that $X_M'' A_1 c_3^{-1}$ will be negative given that $c_3 > 0$. The demand for D is therefore raised by higher risk aversion (p) or return spread on $B(a)$, and lowered by higher mean expected returns on $B(q)$. Since c_7 and $c_4 c_5$ are both negative, the coefficient on r (the own return on D) exerts a positive effect. Qualitatively similar results follow for technical progress that cuts the time devoted to managing D or to higher wealth (since $c_4 c_7 X_M'' > 0$). Technical progress that raises the time savings obtained from money holdings (higher A_1) exerts a negative direct effect on the demand for D, which is likely to swamp the positive indirect effect which results from the parallel induced cut in the demand for B.

The equation for dM reveals that the complex coefficient on wealth is positive and higher wealth brings the expected rise in the demand for money. Since c_1 and c_2 are both negative, money holdings are raised by greater risk aversion or by a greater spread of returns on B. However, it should be pointed out that $c_4 \to 0$ if $X_D'' \to 0$, so that a constant marginal time cost of managing D would mean that changes in a or p were registered in shifts between D and B, leaving M unchanged. The demand for money tends to fall if the return on D increases. The effect of technical progress on the time-saving properties of money (higher A_1) has an ambiguous effect on the demand for it because, on the one hand, it lowers the relative price of liquidity but, at the same time, technical progress means less cash is required per unit of transactions time, that is, the agent requires less cash to achieve the same level of liquidity than prior to the technical progress. Technical progress in the time cost of managing D (lower A_2) or B (lower A_3) reduces the demand for money.

Figures 4.3 to 4.6 show how the efficiency frontier is affected by changes in a selection of parameters. The height of the efficiency frontier is affected by changes in r or q. In Figure 4.3, a rise in r is shown to displace F vertically upwards and an increase in q will raise $EGHJ$, making for a taller box, as illustrated in Figure 4.4. The spread side of the efficiency plane is shifted by a change in the spread parameter, a. Figure 4.5 shows that a fall in a shifts $EKFL$ backward towards the origin. The effect of a change in the technology parameter that enhances liquidity ($dA_1 > 0$) shifts the

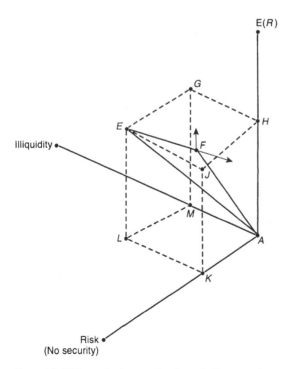

Figure 4.3 Higher r displaces point F vertically upwards.

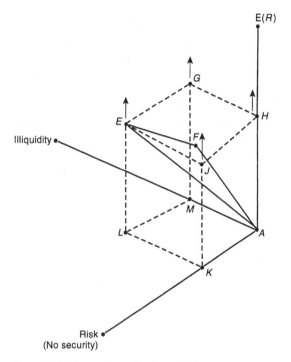

Figure 4.4 Higher *q* raises the plane *EGHJ*.

efficiency plane from *EFA* to EFA_1 (Figure 4.6) to capture a right-ward shift in *A* along the illiquidity axis while retaining zero values for expected return and risk.

4.3.2   Reforms of the London stock market: an application of the model

The results obtained for changes in *B*, *D* and *M* in response to parameter changes permit one to analyse the effects of changes in the regulatory environment for the financial intermediaries that supply *B* and *D*. In the United Kingdom, there have been many regulatory changes since the introduction of Competition and Credit Control in 1971. In this subsection, we concentrate on the impact of reforms of London's stock market. These include 'Big Bang', 1986, and the Financial Services Act, 1986. In addition, the

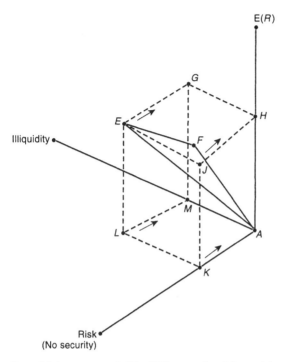

Figure 4.5 Lower spread shifts *EJKL* towards origin on risk axis.

SEAQ[3] Automated Execution Facility (SAEF), introduced in 1989, is a technological change that affected small share dealings on the London Stock Exchange.

The term 'Big Bang' covers a series of reforms that began in April 1982. Using the terminology of Kay and Vickers (1988), the changes altered the structure of the stock market. An important regulatory change was the Financial Services Act, which made it illegal to conduct an unauthorised investment business. The Treasury has delegated the power to authorise firms to the Securities and Investment Board (SIB) and the Self-Regulatory Organisations (SROs).[4] In addition, the SIB and SROs were

---

3 Stock Exchange Automated Quotations.
4 In 1999, the SIB and SROs were merged into the Financial Services Authority (FSA).

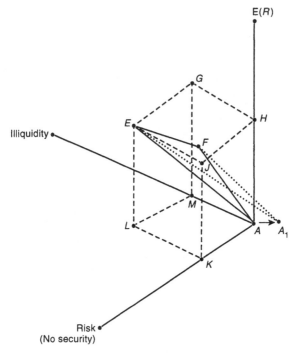

Figure 4.6 $dA_1 > 0$ shifts efficiency plane from *EFA* to *EFA₁*.

given powers to formulate regulations, create compensation schemes, and ensure that regular monitoring and reporting procedures are in place.

Table 4.3 summarises the effects these regulatory and technological changes will have on the parameters derived from the characteristics framework. Consider first the parameter q, the expected return

Table 4.3 The impact of regulatory changes on key parameters

Parameters	q	r	a	A_1, A_3
Big Bang	?	NA	?+	$+A_1, -A_3$
Financial Services Act	−	NA	?+	$+A_1, -A_3$
SAEF	+	NA	?+	$+A_1, -A_3$
Net impact	SR: $+q$	NA	?+	$+A_1, -A_3$
	LR: ?	NA	?+	$+A_1, -A_3$

on B, assumed to be made up of the yield on equities and long-term bonds. SAEF is an automated execution facility for share deals involving 1000 shares or less (50% of the Stock Exchange business) that are quoted on SEAQ. The introduction of SAEF in 1989 should lower the transactions costs for share dealings, and therefore raise q.

The Big Bang reforms that began in April 1982 culminated with a number of changes which took effect in April 1986. Entry restrictions had been gradually eased from April 1982, and in March 1986 free entry of non-exchange member firms was permitted. SEAQ was also introduced, where securities were classified (by liquidity) into alpha, beta, gamma or delta stocks.[5] Market makers were initially required to quote firm two-way prices on alpha and beta securities, and indicative prices for gamma and delta stocks. But in February 1989, the rules were changed: market makers were no longer required to quote firm prices to each other and details of trades of alpha stocks in excess of £100 000 were published the next day.

In October 1986, minimum commissions on Stock Exchange transactions were abolished, and dual capacity dealing in equities was introduced, that is, firms could offer both market-making and stock-broking services. Similar reforms were applied to the gilt-edged market (the market for UK government bonds), which expanded from 3 to 29 market makers.

The impact of Big Bang on q is unclear. Changes which improve the competitive environment, such as the abolition of fixed commissions and increased firm entry, should raise q. For UK equities, the average commission rate fell for all categories of client between 1986 and 1987, except for individuals, where it rose from 0.88% in 1986 to 0.91% in 1987. In many cases, the characteristics of the product offered to clients also changed: firms had withdrawn financial advice on small deals with low commissions.[6]

A London Stock Exchange survey (December 1986) reported significantly lower rates for institutional clients. Over half the transactions in excess of £100 000 were carried out net of commission, though more recent figures point to a revival of agency business.

---

5 In 1991, this was changed to 12 normal market size bands.
6 Observations of this sort point the need to compute price equivalences for nonprice features of financial markets. This is demonstrated in Chapter 5.

Where commission was being charged, average rates were lower than those charged pre-Big Bang, with the differential in average rates between July and December 1986 ranging from 0 to 0.11.

The *touch*, the difference between the best bid and best offer price (expressed as a percentage of the mid-price) on a security, provides one with an indication of price behaviour, as commissions decline in importance. Table 4.4 reports the average spreads pre- and post-Big Bang in the UK equity markets for alpha, beta and gamma stocks. It shows that after Big Bang, average touches fell, especially for beta and gamma stocks. They rose dramatically after the crash of October 1987, and, for alpha stocks, subsequently returned to levels observed after Big Bang. Touches for beta and gamma stocks are still substantially higher than they were in January 1987.

In the gilts market, institutional clients have enjoyed trading net of commission, direct with market makers. Private client commissions declined slightly.

In the short term, therefore, it appears that the impact on q of reforms that were part of Big Bang are positive, except for the private investor. However, the longer-term implications are less clear cut: dual capacity dealing has increased capital requirements for stockbroking firms, and they may also face higher costs if they are to comply with the more stringent regulations imposed by the Financial Services Act.

The '?+' in the a column of Table 4.3 shows that Big Bang, the Financial Services Act and SAEF will have ambiguous, but probably positive effects on the mean preserving spread on q, a. Reforms

Table 4.4 Average touches[a] (%) in the UK equity market

	Alpha	Beta	Gamma
Pre-Big Bang	0.75	1.82	3.37
End 01/87	0.73	1.66	2.91
Pre-crash/87	0.83	1.76	3.00
End 10/87	2.00	3.94	4.95
End 3/88	1.27	3.28	5.48
End 9/88	0.80	2.88	5.00
End 3/89	0.84	2.57	4.76

Source: London Stock Exchange, *Quality of Markets Quarterly*, various issues.

Notes

a Touch: difference between best bid and best offer price among market makers, expressed as a percentage of the mid-price.

of the London Stock Exchange and the Financial Services Act should raise liquidity, and together with SAEF, increase the information flows in bond and equity markets. There is an ongoing debate as to whether more information increases volatility, with attention focused on the October 1987 crash. In a survey of 25 selected exchanges, the London Stock Exchange (1988) concluded that the distinguishing feature of the 1987 crash was the speed of the downturn, most of the decline occurring in a three-day period. The speed of the decline is probably explained by the globalisation of markets and speed of information flows. For example, Bertero and Mayer (1990), in a study of the reactions of 23 stock exchanges to the crash, concluded that information flows are an important determinant of correlations between markets. Thus it is probably fair to conclude that regulatory and technological changes which increase the international competitive environment and information flows increase a, the spread parameter on q.

In the absence of any reliable measure for the technology parameters, A_1 and A_3, one can only speculate as to the effect of regulatory changes. The reforms will improve the competitive environment, demand more information from stockbroking firms and increase the speed with which information becomes available. Therefore, one would expect to observe technical progress associated with M and B, with the consequent effects on the demands for these assets. These reforms will have little direct impact on A_2, the technology parameter associated with deposits.

Finally, in Table 4.3, a 'non-applicable' (NA) term appears in the column for r, the expected return on D. This is because these regulatory reforms are unlikely to have a direct impact on r. However, there are other regulatory changes in the UK financial system which will affect r. For example, the termination of cartel arrangements and increased market entry into retail banking should raise r, as will the introduction of new technology that lowers transactions costs. The technology parameter, A_2, will also be affected. This observation demonstrates the importance of looking at the entire regulatory picture if one is to conduct a proper assessment of the impact of reforms in the characteristics framework.

There are a number of limitations to this simple model. First, the model is atemporal in the sense that agents maximise expected utility for some defined future point in time (or planning horizon) rather than over a sequence or continuum of dates. This simplification fails to capture an important characteristic of certain financial assets or liabilities—that they can transfer spending power over time. Second, the model abstracts from issues of spatial location, where the portability of M (and increasingly, D) can help reduce transactions costs. Third, inflation risk is ignored. Allowing for inflation and indexation could make B a more secure asset than M or unindexed B. Finally, B is treated as a homogeneous asset or liability, which abstracts from the multidimensionality of risky assets differing in such properties as redemption date, currency, tax status and so on. While these simplifications limit the general applicability of the model developed here, it does not prevent the satisfaction of the general objective of this chapter, to define financial products and markets in terms of the characteristics offered by them.

4.3.3 The characteristics model and the firm

The model developed for the household that is a buyer of financial products may be extended to firms which purchase items in the financial markets as part of their production process. Suppose a firm produces a single product that can be sold under competitive conditions for price P. It faces an exogenous rental rate on capital, k, which is also deterministic. Rented capital, K, may be put to the following uses:

M money holdings,
D deposit holdings,
B bond holdings, which may be positive or negative,
Z fixed assets $= K - M - D - B$.

The firm can also hire labour, N, at a given wage of w. Labour may be applied to financial activity (N_f) and to direct production $(N - N_f)$. The firm's output depends on Z and $N - N_f$:

$$Q = f(K - M - D - B, N - N_f)$$

and the production function is well behaved, i.e.

$$f_i, f_{ij} > 0 > f_{ii}; \quad i, j = 1, 2.$$

As in the model of the household, D carries a non-stochastic return r and B a random return, q. Note that B is not constrained to positive quantities: the firm may issue bonds in order to raise capital to finance its activities. In a more complex model, overdraft facilities and other forms of borrowing could be incorporated. Transactions costs for the firm depend on M, D, B and N_f, i.e.

$$t = t(M, D, B, N_f), \quad (t_1, t_4 < 0 < t_3 \quad \text{and} \quad t_2 \gtrless 0).$$

Assume the firm has the objective of maximising some well-defined concave function v of profits. The optimisation problem will be to set K, M, D, B, N and N_f to maximise:

$$\int_{-\infty}^{+\infty} v(PQ - wN - kK - t + rD + qB)f(q)dq \qquad (4)$$

where $f(q)$ is the probability distribution function for the stochastic variable, q. As in the case of the household, the analysis is simplified by specialising $v(\cdot)$ to the negative exponential form and $f(q)$ to the rectangular distribution $[\bar{q} + a/2, \bar{q} - a/2]$. This yields a maximand, the first-order conditions of which are (ignoring corner solutions):

$$Pf_1 = k = -t_1 = r - t_3$$

$$Pf_2 = w = t_4$$

$$q - t_3 = Pf_1 = 1/PB + (a/2)[(1 + e^{apB})/(e^{apB} - 1)].$$

The first equation states that net industrial capital, $K - M - B - D$, is to be raised to the point where the value of its marginal product just balances its rental rate, k. This, in turn, will equal the value of the liquidity services of money holdings $(-t_1)$ and the return, net of liquidity services, from holdings of B. The second equation states that labour is hired to the point where the wage rate w balances both the value of labour's marginal product in production (Pf_2) and the marginal value of its transactions services (t_4). The third equation gives the optimum holdings of B: the expected yield (cost), q, net of liquidity cost t_3 and the value of the capital's marginal product, should be set equal to an expression capturing the risk on this asset (liability).

The function t may be formalised along the same lines as in Section 4.3.1 above on household optimisation, to incorporate a role for technological change. For example, the time cost function t could be defined as:

$$t = -A_1 g_M(M) + A_2 g_D(D) + A_3 g_B(B) + A_4 g_N(N_f)$$

by analogy with that of the household. Technical progress could be captured by rises in A_1 or A_4 and falls in A_3 and (if $g_D > 0$) in A_2. A rise in A_4 would occur if the firm could employ its own labour more productively in the conduct of financial transactions, as a result of, say, improved computer systems. This would lead to an economisation of money balances and perhaps, also, deposit holdings. A rise in A_1, the technology parameter on money holdings, would induce a substitution away from 'in house' financial employment, N_f. A fall in A_3 or A_2 (if $g_D > 0$) would induce a reduction in the portfolio management costs of the firm's interest-bearing assets by inducing substitution away from M and N_f.

The whole system can be differentiated totally to obtain the firm's demand functions for its four assets in rate of change form, together with its associated demand for labour (N), N_f and output supply. Qualitatively similar results on the effects of technical change will emerge, as will the impact of deregulation, increased competition, and so on.

The analysis could be expanded to handle randomness in the firm's product price and capital rental, imperfect competition, taxation and other phenomena. It could also be dynamised to obtain optimal intertemporal behavioural relations for the firm.

4.4 Regulatory and technological changes: the supply side

In Sections 4.2 and 4.3, the case was made for employing the characteristics model in the analysis of financial markets. These sections demonstrated how one could model the demand side of the financial market in order to analyse the impact of regulatory and technological changes. The literature on the supply side of financial markets is comparatively well developed. Existing models could be incorporated into the framework of analysis developed in this chapter. Most important would be the specification of joint production and cost functions for the financial firm. Firms would offer a number of financial products with different combinations of risk, expected return and security. For example, Kim (1986) specifies a multiproduct bank cost function and demonstrates the hazards of representing banking technology if an aggregate measure of output is employed. This type of model could be extended to consider the impact of new technology on the output decisions of financial firms. To capture the impact of regulatory changes, it would be necessary to model different types of market structures, specifying reaction functions in cases of imperfect competition. Future research should be directed to the development of a financial markets model where these points are integrated into a fully specified demand side.

4.5 Conclusion

The purpose of this chapter was to employ the characteristics model to obtain comprehensive definitions of a financial product and a financial market, in the interests of setting applied work on a firm footing. Special attention was paid to the specification of the demand side. A sketch of the supply side was also presented.

In applied work, the conventional approach is to think of the financial sector in broad terms and to concentrate any empirical study on sub-aggregates within this sector. For example, in the United Kingdom, research has focused on sub-sectors such as the securities industry, the building societies, the major clearing banks, and the insurance industry. Also, a somewhat vague concept of a financial market restricts most studies to one country. The characteristics definition of financial product or market frees the applied researcher from these limitations.

Appendix I

The conventional signs of the first-order derivatives of the labour supply and asset demand functions are:

$$h_1^* \gtreqless 0; \quad h_2^* < 0; \quad h_3^* \gtreqless 0; \quad h_4^* \gtreqless 0; \quad h_5^* > 0; \quad h_6^* > 0$$

$$M_1^* > 0; \quad M_2^* \gtreqless 0; \quad M_3^* < 0; \quad M_4^* < 0; \quad M_5^* > 0; \quad M_6^* > 0$$

$$B_1^* < 0; \quad B_2^* \gtreqless 0; \quad B_3^* \gtreqless 0; \quad B_4^* < 0; \quad B_5^* < 0; \quad B_6^* < 0$$

$$D_1^* \gtreqless 0; \quad D_2^* \gtreqless 0; \quad D_3^* > 0; \quad D_4^* \gtreqless 0; \quad D_5^* > 0; \quad D_6^* > 0.$$

Appendix 2

The household's optimisation problem is as follows. The assumption of additive separability in the utility function between leisure time and consumption means the first-order conditions for portfolio efficiency can be identified independently from the wider set of conditions given in Section 4.3 (equations (1)–(3)), that also entail optimisation of the supply of labour. As far as the former conditions are concerned, we find:

$$r = w(t_2 - t_1) \tag{A1}$$

$$(y + 1)/(y - 1) = (2/a)[q - rl + (pB)^{-1}], \tag{A2}$$

where $y = e^{apB}$ and $l = (t_3 - t_1)/(t_2 - t_1)$.

The first of these conditions states that the interest gain on D must balance the value of the marginal cost of the transactions time devoted to asset D, in comparison with M. It therefore gives the optimum trade-off between M and D. The second condition gives the optimum risk–return trade-off between B and the other assets in the portfolio, M and D.

Total differentiation of these last two conditions, and the function for t and its derivatives establishes the demand for B in rate of change form:

$$
\begin{aligned}
c_3 dB = c_1 dp + c_2 da + dq/a &= (dw/aw)(1 + c_4 c_5) \\
&+ (c_4 c_5/a)dr/r - (w/a)[A_1 X_M'' c_4 dw + c_4 c_5 X_D' dA_2 \\
&+ x_B dA_3 + c_4 X_M' dA_1].
\end{aligned}
\tag{A3}
$$

To obtain an equation for a change in the demand for asset D, total differentiation of the condition $r = w(x_2 - x_1)$ implies:

$$
\begin{aligned}
dD = c_6\{(r/w)(dr/r - dw/w) &- X_D' dA_2 - X_M' dA_1 \\
&- X_M'' A_1 [dW - dB]\}.
\end{aligned}
$$

Substitution into the equation for dB establishes that:

$$
\begin{aligned}
dD = c_6\{(X_M'' A_1/c_3)[c_1 dp + c_2 da + dq/a - (w/a)X_B' dA_3] \\
+ (dr/wr)[r + c_4 c_5 c_7] - (dw/w^2)[r - c_7(c_4 c_5 + 1)] \\
- X_M' dA_1[1 + c_4 c_7] - X_D' dA_2[1 + c_4 c_5 c_7] \\
- A_1 X_M'' dW[1 + A_1 X_M'' c_4 c_7]\}.
\end{aligned}
\tag{A4}
$$

In the above three equations, the following definitions are employed:

$$c_1 = yaB(y - 1)^{-2} - (apB^2)^{-1}$$

$$c_2 = (y - 1)^{-1}[ypB/(y - 1) - (y + 1)/2a]$$

$$c_3 = (apB^2)^{-1} - apy(y - 1)^{-2} + (w/a)[X_B'' A_3 - X_M'' A_1 c_4]$$

$$c_4 = [1 - (X_M'' A_1 / X_D'' A_2)]^{-1}$$

$$c_5 = X_M'' A_1 / X_D'' A_2$$

$$c_6 = (X_D'' A_2 - X_M'' A_1)^{-1}$$

$$c_7 = X_M'' A_1 w / a c_3.$$

Lastly, changes in the demand for money, dM, can be obtained from the portfolio identity $W = M + D + B$, which implies that: $dM = dW - dB - dD$. Substitution for dB and dD gives:

$$\begin{aligned}
dM = {}& dW\{1 + c_4[c_7 + c_5(1 + A_1 X_M'' c_4 c_7)]\} \\
& - (c_4/c_3)[c_1 dp + c_2 da + dq/a - w/a X_B' dA_3] \\
& - (dw/w)\{(c_4 c_5 + 1)/ac_3 + c_6/w[r - c_7(c_4 c_5 + 1)]\} \\
& - (dr/r)[(c_4 c_5/ac_3 + 1/w)r + c_4 c_5 c_7)]\} \\
& + X_M' dA_1[wc_4/ac_3 + c_6(1 + c_4 c_7)] \\
& + X_D' dA_2[wc_4 c_5/ac_3 + c_6(1 + c_4 c_5 c_7)].
\end{aligned} \quad (A5)$$

References

Arrow, K. (1964). The role of securities in the optimal allocation of risk bearing. *Review of Economic Studies*, 31, 91–96.

Bertero, E. and Mayer, C. (1990). Structure and performance: Global interdependence of stock markets around the crash of October 1987. *European Economic Review*, 34, 1155–80.

Kane, E. J. (1981). Accelerating inflation, technological innovation and the decreasing effectiveness of banking regulation. *Journal of Finance*, 36, 355–67.

Kane, E. J. (1983). Policy implications of structural changes in financial markets. *American Economic Review*, 73, 96–100.

Kay, J. and Vickers, J. (1988). Regulatory reform in Britain. *Economic Policy*, 7, 286–351.

Kim, M. (1986). Banking technology and the existence of a consistent output aggregate. *Journal of Monetary Economics*, 18, 181–95.

London Stock Exchange (1988). World stock exchanges: Responses to the crash. *Quality of Markets Quarterly*, Summer.

Silber, W. L. (1975). *Financial Innovations*. Lexington: D.C. Heath.

Silber, W. L. (1983). The process of financial innovation. *American Economic Review*, 73, 89–95.

Stiglitz, J. E. and Weiss, A. (1981). Credit rationing in markets with imperfect information. *American Economic Review*, 71, 393–410.

Stiglitz, J. E. and Weiss, A. (1983). Incentive effects of terminations: Applications to the credit and labor markets. *American Economic Review*, 73, 912–27.

Chapter 5

The computation of interest equivalences for the nonprice characteristics of bank products

Shelagh A. Heffernan

Financial products have many nonprice characteristics that consumers value. We show that the characteristics model provides a useful framework both for quantifying these nonprice characteristics and for converting them to interest equivalences. The principal advantage of this approach is that it keeps the key characteristics small in number. The model is applied to a range of UK retail bank products.

5.1 Introduction

For a number of financial products, their nonprice characteristics may be as important as their price. In the case of stockbroking services, analysts' advice and soft commissions feature prominently, in addition to commission rates. In retail banking, characteristics such as branch size, automatic teller machine (ATM) access and service charges are, among other factors, integral parts of the retail product offered to customers. If one wishes to assess competitive behaviour in financial markets, it is important to 'price' these characteristics and adjust the price of the product accordingly.

There have been several theoretical contributions to the concept of implicit interest. Feige (1964) treated US bank service charges as negative interest. Klein (1974) assumed fully competitive implicit interest rates and entered these rates in a money demand function. He found the implicit interest rate variable to be significant and of nearly equal magnitude (but opposite in sign) to the yields on alternative assets. Mitchell (1979) used a model to establish the

Reprinted from *Journal of Money, Credit and Banking*, Vol. 24, No. 2, pp. 162–72, May 1992. Copyright 1992 by Ohio State University Press. All rights reserved.

conditions under which banks treat explicit and implicit interest (in the form of cheque-clearing services) as substitutes. His main point was that explicit and implicit rates may move together depending on the degree of substitutability between deposit and chequing accounts. There are also numerous empirical contributions in this area, all of which have employed US data. These are cited throughout the chapter, where appropriate.

This chapter seeks to achieve two objectives. The first is to develop a methodology to test for the significance of nonprice characteristics of bank products, and the second is to apply this methodology to a selection of British retail bank products: the higher-interest deposit account (HID), the higher-interest chequing account (HIC), repayment mortgages (RM) and personal loans (PL).

The British retail banking industry is a good choice for applying and testing this methodology because a number of reforms aimed at encouraging greater competition in this sector have given rise to a proliferation of nonprice features associated with relatively new retail bank products. Prior to the first regulatory change in 1971,[1] the industry was dominated by four large clearing banks, some smaller banks, and what at the time were largely savings banks, the Trustee Savings Banks and the National Girobank. Building societies, as mutual organisations offering services exclusively related to the housing market, were not considered retail banks because they did not offer personal loans or money transmission facilities. By the late 1980s, the structure of retail banking had undergone a dramatic change. Banks had moved into the mortgage market and the largest building societies (in terms of asset size) were retail banks in all but name, offering mortgages, personal loans, a variety of deposit products, chequing facilities and cash-dispensing machines. Indeed in 1989, Abbey National, the largest building society, took advantage of the 1986 Building Society Act and became a bank.

One consequence of these changes was the development of new financial products and an increase in nonprice features associated with these products. Examples include the HIC and HID accounts, introduced in 1984 and 1985, respectively. HIC offers substantially higher interest rates than the standard '7-day' deposit account. While personal loans have been offered by banks for a long period,

---

1 Competition and Credit Control.

building societies began to enter this market in early 1987. Banks entered the mortgage market in 1981, traditionally the exclusive domain of the building societies. The repayment mortgage, one of the products considered in this chapter, is one of two major types of mortgage offered in the United Kingdom. It is distinguished from the endowment mortgage in that it does not have an endowment assurance policy attached to it.

This chapter is divided into five sections. Section 5.2 outlines the methodology for identifying and 'pricing' the important nonprice characteristics of British bank products. Section 5.3 discusses the construction of the data series used in the estimation work. Section 5.4 reviews the results of the estimation exercises and Section 5.5 explains how interest equivalences are computed. Section 5.6 concludes.

5.2 Methodology

A number of empirical studies have attempted to estimate an implicit rate of interest. All of these studies employ US banking data and tend to focus on bank products where, during the estimating period, no explicit interest was paid. Klein and Murphy (1971) used bank service charges as a measure of implicit yield on demand deposits that were prohibited from earning an explicit interest. Barro and Santomero (1972) computed service charge remissions as a measure of implicit interest, for a chequing account with no explicit interest. Data were drawn from a survey of large commercial banks. Santomero (1979) constructed an implicit interest rate series using the Functional Cost Analysis Program of the Federal Reserve which is based on bank survey data and provides direct information on the costs of servicing non-interest-paying demand deposits. Implicit interest was computed for one nonprice feature, service costs. Total costs were assumed linear in three activities, demand deposits, time deposits and loans. Having obtained a measure of implicit interest, it was regressed on $(1 - c)r_a$, where r_a is the yield on the alternative asset and c is reserves plus float. Based on pooled time-series/cross-section data from 1973–75, Santomero concluded that implicit interest was being paid at one-third to one-half the competitive rate. Becker (1975) defined and computed the net rate of return on demand deposits as the value of services rendered by banks (non-interest expenses per dollar) less any service charges per dollar of demand deposits.

Startz (1983) estimated the implicit interest from the provision of free banking services. The implicit return on the demand deposit account was based on estimates from Barro and Santomero (1972), Becker (1975) and Klein (1974). Also included as a dependent variable was the fixed cost of maintaining the account at the bank per unit of time *t*. In a regression where demand deposits was the dependent variable, Startz found the coefficients for implicit return, opportunity costs, real income and lagged demand deposit balances were statistically significant with the correct sign.

The methodology employed in this chapter differs from the past literature in a number of respects. In the United Kingdom, equivalent functional cost data of the sort provided by the Federal Reserve are not available, hence the need to construct the data series described in Section 5.3 below. In addition, by the mid-1980s, most retail deposit products paid an explicit rate of interest. There continues to exist a current account that pays no interest, but the consumer can choose a superior product in the HIC account, which has all the features of the current account and pays interest. Service charges do not apply, except for certain categories of overdraft customers. Thus, explicit interest and nonprice characteristics are not mutually exclusive.

In this chapter, the product interest rate is regressed on market interest rates (current and lagged) and the nonprice characteristics of bank products, with the objective of identifying explanatory variables that are statistically significant. The equation, estimated by ordinary least squares (OLS), takes the following form:

$$r = a + \sum_{i=1}^{n} b_i x_i + c_0 LIBOR + \sum_{i=1}^{2} c_i LIBOR_{-i} + eTT + u_i \quad (1)$$

where

$\quad\quad\quad r =$ the rate of interest offered/levied by a bank on the product
$\quad\quad\quad x_i = i$th nonprice characteristic x, $i = 1, \ldots, n$
$\quad LIBOR =$ the three-month sterling London interbank offered rate
$LIBOR_{-i} = LIBOR$ lagged by i, $i = 1, 2$ months
$\quad\quad\quad TT =$ time trend
$\quad\quad\quad u_i =$ error term.

This equation is estimated on a pooled time-series/cross-section data set (described in Section 5.4) for the HIC account, the HID account, and pooled interest rates for the products for HIC and HID (HICD). In addition, repayment mortgages and personal loans (RMPL) were pooled in order to estimate interest certainty equivalences, such as the mortgage condition that the borrower offer security as insurance against the possibility of default. Coefficients on correctly signed, statistically significant explanatory variables are used to compute an interest equivalence for each nonprice characteristic.

5.3 Constructing the data series

Data for this study come from an unpublished source, one of the major clearing banks in the United Kingdom. The bank collects the following information on itself, other banks, and the large building societies: (1) Monthly information on interest rates offered/levied on retail bank products in the United Kingdom. The series goes as far back as 1976 but for the purposes of this study, the observation period runs from 1 August 1985 to 1 November 1989, depending on the bank product. It is not a consistent monthly series, the interest sheet normally being updated only if there is a change in a central bank rate. Rates used in this study are net of composite rate tax for the deposit products and are annual percentage loan rates for the loan products. Deposit rates are annual rates, unless otherwise stated, that is, unless the interest on the deposit is paid more than once a year. (2) An annual or twice-annual summary of the nonprice features of these bank products.

This information permitted the construction of a pooled time-series/cross-section database on interest rates and nonprice features for a number of products. For the purpose of this study, data on HIC and HID accounts, repayment mortgages and personal loans are used.

Interest rates and other characteristics for HIC and HID accounts vary according to deposit levels, which range from £0 to over £53 000. Initially, a series was created for 11 deposit levels, ranging from £96 to £53 000. These deposit levels were chosen in such a way that they were in the middle range, to avoid being close to interest rate threshold kinks, where there is a sudden jump in the interest rate offered as a consequence of the size of the deposit rising by some small amount. The deposit levels were also deflated by a quarterly money GDP deflator. Related work by the author (Heffernan 1993) revealed similar trends across deposit levels and for the purposes of this study, we concentrate on two deposit levels: D4 (£765) and D6 (£4590). These correspond to the average deposit levels for, respectively, current accounts and deposit accounts in the late 1980s.

This exercise generated 40 interest rate points for HIC and HID, from 1 August 1985 to 1 November 1989, at two deposit levels, D4 and D6. The number of financial institutions included in the sample ranged from six to 11 for HID and from four to 11 for HIC. The sample of financial institutions tended to be smaller for the earlier observation points because fewer of them offered these products.

For mortgages and personal loans, it was not necessary to specify a loan amount because banks and building societies tend to quote one interest rate that does not vary with the size of the loan. They do set minimum and maximum amounts, and these were included as nonprice features of bank loans. The interest rate series constructed for banks and personal loans was from 1 June 1986 to 1 November 1989, giving a total of 32 interest rate points for each firm. The number of firms in the sample varied from 10 to 12 for mortgages, and from three to 16 for personal loans. In the early part of the period, fewer firms offered these products, especially personal loans.

Information on the nonprice characteristics of these products was compiled once or twice a year. It was assumed that in the interval between reporting dates, the characteristics were unchanged. The monthly product interest rate was associated with the set of characteristics reported closest to that month. There are a number of characteristics common to all institutions. For example, they tend to offer the same service in the provision of account statements. Nonprice features of products common to all the institutions in the sample were eliminated. The series created was based on characteristics that showed substantial differences between institutions.

For the HIC account the characteristics included the following: a minimum investment requirement (MI); a minimum deposit requirement (MD); a minimum cheque constraint (MC), where the customer is constrained to write cheques for values in excess of some minimum amount; the number of branches for the firm offering the product ($BRAN$); the number of times interest is paid in a given year ($INTPAID$); and the number of automatic teller machines available (*ATM*). The branch variable is included as a proxy for other nonprice and near-bank features an institution may offer, such as convenience of location, retail stockbroking services, and foreign exchange facilities. In the UK, it is the larger branch banks (especially the big four clearing banks) that offer these sorts of services. Nelson (1985, 1988) showed the theoretical and empirical importance of the dimension of 'convenience' for bank costs and market structure in retail banking. For the HID account the nonprice characteristics include *MI*, *BRAN*, *INTPAID*, a maximum withdrawal (*MW*) constraint (a customer may only withdraw a specified maximum amount in a given day or week), and *NOTICE*, whether or not notice of withdrawal is required.

Data from the HIC and HID were pooled at the two deposit levels, with the objective of establishing an interest equivalence for chequing facilities, the key feature that differentiates these two products. The aggregated product is called HICD (D4 and D6) and includes the following characteristics: a cheque dummy (*CHQ*), *MI*, *MW*, *BRAN*, *INTPAID*, *NOTICE* and *ATM*.

Data for repayment mortgages and personal loans (RMPL) were pooled and a security dummy inserted. Since security is required for mortgages (the bank holds the title deeds to the house) but not for personal loans, the dummy allows one to estimate an interest equivalence for security. Similarly for insurance (the borrower is required to take out insurance to cover the mortgage repayments in the event of death), though a 0.5 dummy is inserted to allow for optional insurance, where applicable. In addition, the minimum and maximum amount available for loans (*MIN, MAX*), minimum and maximum terms (*MINT, MAXT*) and number of branches are included.

The list of nonprice characteristics used is by no means exhaustive. For example, it is known that at least two banks offer some form of home banking, but this feature is excluded from the list. The study was limited by data availability because only a selection of nonprice features was reported. However, the information was gathered by a major clearing bank, and one would expect that it was interested in nonprice features it thought to be the most important from the standpoint of its business strategy. In addition, it is only possible to include characteristics that showed a high degree of variability between banks. Another concern relates to the extent to which pooling is acceptable within this model. There is pooling over months, institutions, and over two types of product, mortgages and personal loans.

5.4   Results

Equation (1) was estimated using OLS. The R^2 ranges from 0.6871 to 0.9599. The adjusted R^2 was not very different from the unadjusted R^2.

One concern is the possibility of serial correlation, since the interest rate on financial products change only when there is a change in the central bank rate. The Durbin–Watson (DW) tests show the null hypothesis of no autocorrelation cannot be rejected for most of the products, while for the other products, a Lagrange multiplier test for higher autocorrelation allows us to accept the null hypothesis at both the 1% and 5% significance levels.

The presence of heteroscedasticity is another concern given the cross-sectional nature of the data. The Lagrange multiplier test for heteroscedasticity was used, where the null hypothesis is that the disturbances have a constant variance. It was tested for significance at both the 1% and 5% levels using the F distribution. For the deposit products, the null hypothesis of homoscedasticity cannot be rejected at the 1% and 5% significance levels, but for loan products, heteroscedasticity problems meant only the estimates from one subset of the 1988 pooled RMPL product could be used with any confidence.

For the higher-interest chequing account HIC4, the following variables were found to be statistically significant with the correct sign: $LIBOR$, minimum investment (MI) and the number of branches ($BRAN$). The t-ratio for minimum deposit (MD) is nearly significant with the correct sign. At deposit level six (£4590) (HIC6), $LIBOR$, $LIBOR_{-2}$, MD and branches are statistically significant with the expected sign. The constant term (CON) is insignificant for HIC4 but negative and significant for HIC6. The ATM variable (number of ATMs) is statistically significant for HIC4 and HIC6 but the sign is positive at D4 and negative at D6.

For the HID account, the following explanatory variables were found to be correctly signed and statistically significant for HID6: $LIBOR$, $LIBOR_{-2}$, MI, branches, maximum withdrawal (MW) and the number of times interest is paid in a given year ($INTPAID$). Required notice of withdrawal ($NOTICE$) is significant but is incorrectly signed. The time trend (TT) is negative and significant, suggesting that interest rates are falling over time. The constant term is positive and significant. Similar results are obtained for HID6 except that MW and the number of branches are no longer significant at this higher deposit level.

The ATM variable is difficult to interpret. On the one hand, it is a characteristic that eases consumer access to deposit funds, and using this reasoning, it should have a negative sign: the provision of ATM facilities lowers the interest rate offered on the product, as it appears to do for HIC6. On the other hand, it is a piece of technology which, if used instead of a cheque or a withdrawal from a cashier-attended counter, reduces the cost of money transmission for banks. In this case, we would expect a positive sign, as we observe for HIC4, HID4 and HID6. Van der Velde (1985) of the Bank Administration Institute, using US data, found that ATMs have a largely neutral effect on bank costs, because although costs per transaction are lower when compared to a full teller service, customers use the ATM more often, thereby raising overall costs. This point is supported by a recent survey of large US banks, which found that automation technology is offered to provide a better service rather than to reduce costs (*The American Banker*, 6 October 1990). Unfortunately, similar information on British ATM costs does not exist.

Turning to the aggregated product, HICD, all the variables tested are significant with the expected sign with the exception of $LIBOR_{-1}$, $NOTICE$, ATM and the HIC time trend ($TT2$) at D4 and $LIBOR_{-1}$, MW, $INTPAID$, $NOTICE$ and $TT2$ at D6. These results do not mean very much since this is a synthetic product. However, the cheque dummy (1 for HIC, 0 for HID) is statistically significant with a negative sign, that is, if a chequing facility is offered, the interest rate falls.

For the period data on repayment mortgages and personal loans, the presence of heteroscedasticity means attention is confined to the 1988 coefficients. The insurance and security dummies ($INSURANCE$, SEC) and the number of branches are statistically significant with the expected sign.

For most deposit products, $LIBOR$ and $LIBOR_{-2}$ lagged by two months were statistically significant suggesting that, in general, there is a substantial lag in the responsiveness of deposit rates to a change in the market rate of interest. The 1988 pooled mortgage/personal loan product had a statistically significant $LIBOR_{-1}$ but an insignificant $LIBOR$. Recall that in most cases, the constant term is positive and significant. These findings are suggestive of 'smoothing' by the banks; that is, they adjust interest rates slowly and in discrete jumps. There are several possible explanations for smoothing including the presence of menu and/or switching costs or price-making behaviour. Heffernan (1993) explores the competitive behaviour of the British retail banking industry in more detail.

5.5 Computation of interest equivalences

The coefficients from the OLS regressions enable us to compute interest equivalences for the nonprice features of bank products found to be statistically significant with the expected sign. These are reported in Table 5.1 for HIC and HID at deposit levels D4 (£765) and D6 (£4590). Results for the 1988 pooled repayment mortgage and personal loan set are reported in Table 5.2. Recall that the interest rate is an annual rate, unless interest is paid to customers more than once a year, a practice picked up by the nonprice characteristic, *INTPAID*. Hence the coefficients on the nonprice features give us a direct measure of the interest sacrificed or obtained as a result of the presence of a positive or negative nonprice characteristic.

The results are best interpreted by considering some examples. The coefficients on the branch variable tell us that as the number of branches increases, the interest offered on the deposit falls. In 1989, the average branch size for the big four clearing banks was 2477. Table 5.1 informs the consumer that for HID, up to 3.2% interest could be forgone at the lower deposit level because of the choice of a bank with an extensive branch network. On the other hand, the customer who could deposit £4590 would lose only 0.003% in interest if the no-branch bank is chosen. On average, the interest forgone is 0.75% at deposit level 4 and 0.01% at deposit level 6. For the HIC account, the average interest sacrificed is between 0.1% and 0.3%, depending on the deposit level.

The number of times interest is paid on a HID account (one, two or four times a year) was found to be significant, and the interest sacrificed ranges between 0.09% and 1.7%. ATMs add to interest paid on HID, but at the higher deposit level for HIC, the consumer actually loses interest because of the ATM facility.

The summation rows in Table 5.1 provide the reader with an idea of the overall interest lost/gained as a result of the presence of nonprice characteristics. For HID, the consumer loses an average of 1.1% at deposit level 4 and 0.7% at the higher deposit level. The

Table 5.1 Interest equivalences for deposit products

	Interest equivalence[a]		
	Min (%)	Max (%)	Avg (%)
Higher-interest deposit account			
(1) Minimum investment (£0–£1000)			
D4 = £765	0.02	1.12	0.54
D6 = £4590	0.006	0.26	0.15
(2) Maximum withdrawal			
D4 = £765	−0.75	−0.45	−0.66
D6 = £4590	na	na	na
(3) Number of branches (0 to 20 954)			
D4 = £765	−3.2	−0.2	−0.75
D6 = £4590	−0.04	−0.003	−0.01
(4) Interest paid (1, 2 or 4 times per year)			
D4 = £765	−1.7	−0.14	−0.28
D6 = £4590	−1.1	−0.09	−0.23
(5) Number of ATMs (0 to 2700)			
D4 = £765	0	0.6	0.05
D6 = £4590	0	0.3	0.02
(6) Sum [(1) + (2) + (3) + (4) + (5)]			
D4 = £765	−5.6	0.9	−1.1
D6 = £4590	−1.1	0.5	−0.7
Higher-interest chequing (HIC) account			
(1) Minimum investment (£0 to £2500)			
D4 = £765	0	2.4	1.71
D6 = £4590	na	na	na
(2) Minimum deposit (£0 to £250)			
D4 = £765	0	0.3	0.07
D6 = £4590	0	0.46	0.09
(3) Number of branches (0 to 3062)			
D4 = £765	−0.2	0	−0.1
D6 = £4590	−0.5	−0.01	−0.3
(4) Number of ATMs (0 to 2700)			
D4 = £765	0	0.6	0.09
D6 = £4590	−0.6	0	−0.1
(5) Sum [(1) + (2) + (3) + (4)]			
D4 = £765	−0.2	3.3	1.8
D6 = £4590	−1.1	0.5	−0.3
(6) Chequing facility	No cheque	Cheque	
D4 = £765	0	−1.2	
D6 = £4590	0	−0.4	

Note

a An interest equivalence is the interest earned (forgone) because of the presence of a non-price characteristic in a product that is, from the standpoint of the consumer, negative (positive). It is obtained from the statistically significant correctly signed coefficients of the estimates of equation (1). Minimum interest equivalence (Min) is the smallest amount of interest gained or forgone because of the nonprice characteristic, maximum interest equivalence (Max) is the greatest amount gained or lost, and 'Avg' is the average interest equivalence.

Table 5.2 Interest equivalences for loan products (RMPL^a)

(1) Number of branches (0 to 21 071)				
0–104	0–829	0–1546	0–3086	0–21 071
0.055%	0.15%	0.20%	0.29%	0.75%
(2) Insurance (0 = no insurance, 1 = insurance, 0.5 = insurance option)				
0	1	0.5		
0	−2.09%	−1.05%		
(3) Security (0 = no security required, 1 = security required)				
0	1			
0	−7.80%			

Note
a Based on 1988 pooled data for repayment mortgages and personal loans (RMPL).

respective average nominal rates of interest over the period were
7.15% and 7.43% respectively. On average, the consumer gains
1.8% as a result of nonprice characteristics associated with the
HIC account at the lower deposit level and loses 0.3% at deposit
level 6. However, the provision of chequing facilities will increase
the amount of interest forgone on this type of account. Average
nominal rates of interest offered on HIC over the period were
6.57% at deposit level 4 and 7.33% at deposit level 6.

Table 5.2, for loan products, is far more limited in the information it can provide because it is based on pooled 1988 data. The
presence of security on the loan will reduce the interest rate charged
by 7.8%. Insurance will lower it by 2.1%, and the option of insurance (under the heading 0.5) reduces it by just over 1%. Note that
the interest contribution made by branch size is much smaller than
for deposit products, ranging from 0.05% to 0.29% for banks with
branches that range from 1546 to 3086. Over the period, the average
nominal interest rate for repayment mortgages was 11.6% and
20.86% for personal loans.

5.6   Conclusion

In this chapter, we have sought to identify interest equivalences for
the nonprice characteristics of British retail bank products. It differs
from earlier studies in that it relies on UK data, constructs a data
series with both explicit interest and nonprice characteristics, and
uses this database to obtain statistically significant coefficients
that can be employed to compute interest equivalences. Nonprice
characteristics found to be important were the levels of minimum

investment, minimum deposit and maximum withdrawal. The number of branches, ATM outlets, the frequency with which interest is paid and the provision of a chequing facility were also correctly signed and statistically significant.

The findings in this chapter are useful because they permit one to adjust explicit interest for these interest equivalences. This in turn will provide a more accurate measure of price behaviour in retail banking markets. A similar methodology could be applied to financial products in other markets, such as stockbroking services.

However, the greatest constraint to this approach lies in gathering the appropriate data for the estimation procedures, especially information on the nonprice characteristics associated with retail bank products.

References

Barro, R. J. and Santomero, A. M. (1972). Household money holdings and the demand deposit rate. *Journal of Money, Credit and Banking*, 4, 397–413.

Becker, W. E. (1975). Determinants of the US currency-demand deposit ratio. *Journal of Finance*, 30, 57–74.

Feige, E. L. (1964). *The Demand for Liquid Assets: A Temporal Cross Section Analysis*. Englewood Cliffs, N.J.: Prentice-Hall.

Heffernan, S. A. (1993). Competition in British retail banking. *Journal of Financial Services Research*, 7, 309–32.

Klein, B. (1974). Competitive interest payments on banks' deposits and the long-run demand for money. *American Economic Review*, 64, 931–49.

Klein, M. A. and Murphy, N. B. (1971). The pricing of bank deposits: A theoretical and empirical analysis. *Journal of Financial and Quantitative Analysis*, 6, 747–61.

Mitchell, D. W. (1979). Implicit interest on demand deposits. *Journal of Monetary Economics*, 5, 343–64.

Nelson, R. W. (1985). Branching, scale economies, and banking costs. *Journal of Banking and Finance*, 9, 13–23.

Nelson, R. W. (1988). Optimal banking structure: Implications for interstate banking. *Contemporary Policy Issues*, 6, 13–23.

Santomero, A. M. (1979). The role of transactions costs and rates of return on the demand deposit decision. *Journal of Monetary Economics*, 5, 343–64.

Startz, R. (1983) Competition and interest rate ceilings in commercial banking. *Quarterly Journal of Economics*, 98, 255–65.

van der Velde, M. (1985). *ATM Cost Model*. Rolling Meadows, Ill.: Bank Administration Institute.

Chapter 6

A characteristics analysis of financial innovations in short-term retail financial products

Meghnad Desai and William Low

The characteristics model is used to investigate the introduction of interest-bearing time deposit accounts by different financial institutions in the UK. We show that the incentive to innovate by the different institutions is associated with 'gaps' in characteristics space, where the two key characteristics are yield and access. These gaps are quantified in terms of the 'angles' separating the locations of the different accounts in characteristics space. Over time the maximum angle falls, indicating that the process of financial innovation is successful in filling the gaps in characteristics space.

6.1 Introduction

There has been extensive writing on financial innovation in recent years at both the academic and policy-making levels (Silber, 1975, 1983; Federal Reserve Board of New York, 1981–82; Bank of England, 1983). If we take Silber (1983) as a convenient starting point, we see that, as far as the causes of financial innovations are concerned, the main ones are:

1 Policy: existing regulations or legislative initiatives to relax regulations.
2 Inflation and uncertainty: the level and volatility of nominal and real interest rates.

Reprinted from 'Measuring the opportunity for product innovation', in *Changing Money* (M. De Cecco, ed.), © 1987, with permission from Blackwell Publishers, Oxford.

3 Technological change: the introduction of new electronic and telecommunication facilities.
4 Internationalisation: increasing integration of global financial markets.

But while these causes are important, they are still only proximate ones. Even now we have only begun to scratch the surface of the question of the origins, diffusion and implications of financial innovation.

The focus in this chapter is on the microeconomics of financial innovation. The precise question we ask is: *what are the reasons that motivate the suppliers of financial services to innovate?* An early approach to answering this question was made by Greenbaum and Heywood (1973). They look at assets as combinations of characteristics, but having defined the problem, they do not use the characteristics model subsequently in their study. This model is, however, a fruitful starting point, as shown in Chapter 3.

Our focus, in particular, is on the retail deposit market, which covers those financial instruments in which households place their surplus funds on a short-term basis. The financial innovations in which we are interested take the form of:

1 The introduction of new financial instruments in which individuals could place their money.
2 The emergence of new financial institutions which supply instruments/services not provided by existing financial institutions.

Examples of both are easy to provide. There are indexed bonds, NOW deposits, cheque-save accounts, money market accounts, etc., as far as recently introduced assets are concerned. As far as new institutions are concerned, we have seen the entry of non-banking, even nonfinancial, firms into the market for providing financial services—travel agencies/credit card companies such as American Express, stockbrokers such as Merrill Lynch, and retail outlets such as Virgin and Marks & Spencer.

At the outset it should be said that the very existence of these two forms of innovation tells us something about the nature of the financial services industry. Ideally there should only be the first type (type 1 above). It should be possible for existing firms to provide new instruments to meet consumer needs if they are dynamic and competitive enough. If existing firms are not providing services for which a latent demand exists, then this can either be due to regulations preventing them from doing so or because they may be in a 'cosy oligopoly' situation whereby they do not perceive the need to meet the latent demand. In such a case, new firms may move into the market and fill the gap that exists.

This process of a latent demand existing and new products/new firms responding to fill the gap in the existing product mix is what we shall attempt to formulate and measure. Although it is a commonplace occurrence, it turns out to be quite difficult to analyse. Let us illustrate some of the problems.

The first problem concerns the identification of an innovation. In oligopolistic markets with product differentiation, it is a standard selling strategy to describe products as 'new and improved'. A handful of firms, each providing a similar if not identical range of products, may continuously announce new, improved, super versions of their products which may only be new in trivial aspects of product design. It is difficult for an outside observer to judge whether a 'new' toothpaste is new or just has a coloured stripe added to the old ingredients. The US automobile industry in the 1950s and 1960s provides a good example of this phenomenon. A small number of automobile manufacturing firms competed in producing new models of a similar product range year after year, but these improvements were merely in style. It was only when European car makers such as Volkswagen appeared on the US scene that it became obvious that in terms of fuel efficiency there had been no improvement over the years in the US cars. What we need then is some distinction between 'important' innovations and 'trivial' innovations. A bank providing its customers with cheque books in different colours may claim to be innovative, but it is only when a rival bank or nonbank offers higher interest rates for the same withdrawal facility that one would say that we have an important innovation. This implies, of course, an ordering of characteristics by their importance. Such an ordering may be revealed by consumer preference, but this is not guaranteed.

In terms of our analysis, we would define an important innovation as one that locates and fills a gap in the range of available products. Such a gap should be definable in terms of the most important product characteristics. An innovation will also sometimes activate a characteristic that may hitherto have been latent, e.g. fuel efficiency in cars.

The second problem therefore is to measure gaps in the product range. Innovations will be considered to be trivial if the gap in the product range persists despite these trivial innovations occurring. The key concept is the existence and identifiability of a significant gap as a proxy for latent demand.

To identify such gaps is not easy, of course. If one accepts the concepts of consumer sovereignty and perfect markets, such gaps, *by definition*, could not exist. Firms that indulge in trivial innovations can point to consumer satisfaction in the sense that their new products are bought and they are profitable. They may also point to the intense competition they face from rivals who are also producing similar trivial innovations. If one particular car manufacturer did not produce new style car models each year, it would definitely lose its market share. Demand for fuel-efficient, safe, durable cars was very latent in the 1950s and emerged into view only when VW began to penetrate the US market successfully. Even then, it was only after the oil price rises in the 1970s that the European and Japanese car makers began to penetrate the US market seriously.

A third problem, apart from the two of separating trivial from important innovations and identifying latent demand, is the lack of an adequate theoretical framework in which to pose the problem. Even the theory of industrial innovations is in its infancy. There is a small but growing body of work on research and development strategies and the decisions of firms whether to innovate or not, but there are significant differences between industrial and financial products which need to be borne in mind in choosing a framework:

1 A most important difference is that there are no production function-type considerations in introducing new financial instruments, although these are crucial in industrial product innovation. At its basic level, the financial instrument is a contract written on paper and potentially all possible financial contracts can be written without any technological barrier. In this sense, financial innovations are not *new* goods. They are implicitly always there, but in zero supply (see also Greenbaum and Heywood, 1973).

2 Financial instruments are difficult if not impossible to patent. Like other services/goods whose main content is information, once a financial instrument has been launched it is open to quick and almost costless imitation.

3   Although there are no technological considerations, there are tremendous economies of scale. Once a financial intermediary launches a new financial instrument, its profitability will depend crucially on how many people buy that instrument. This is for two reasons. First is the fact that the intermediary's return depends on the yield he pays to his customers for funds and the yield earned by lending out those funds. In wholesale markets, the larger the sum and the longer it can be lent out, the higher the earned yield. Second is the fact that the greater the number of customers, the greater the pool of money for long-term lending, since the risk of a sudden withdrawal of a substantial portion of the pool falls as the number of customers rises (see again Greenbaum and Heywood, 1973).

4   Given the absence of technological considerations, the only factor costs of launching a new financial instrument are the costs of product development, advertising, etc. Since most financial intermediaries are multiproduct firms in this respect, the production costs of a new product launched or the current operating costs of particular instruments can be neglected.

With this background in mind, we proceed in the next section to pose the question of how product innovation and opportunities for product innovation can be measured in the financial markets.

6.2   A characteristics framework

We need to do two things. First, we need to find a way of identifying and measuring the gaps in the range of available products in the financial market that will indicate the potential opportunity for creating and launching new products: this will be an *ex ante* measure. Second, we need to find an *ex post* measure of whether a financial innovation, of an important rather than a trivial sort, has occurred.

There is an extensive discussion in location theory which seems to be a fruitful starting point for our purposes (see, e.g., Rosen, 1974; also Lancaster, 1982, and the other papers contained in that issue of the *Journal of Industrial Economics*). The location of firms existing at any point in time could be described in terms of proximity to each other or in terms of proximity to the consumer. It would then be easy to visualise a gap in the market if existing shops are too far apart in some sense. A potential entrant could locate his shop in the gap if he could calculate *ex ante* that such a location would be profitable.

Using the analogy of physical space, we take the characteristics space as our starting point. Let us begin with the simplest case of a two-characteristics space. As we shall see later, the higher-dimensional case creates many problems.

Let there be two characteristics, R and A. For financial instruments we shall think of return (yield) (R) and access (liquidity) (A) as the two main characteristics. In Figure 6.1, yield (R) is measured along the vertical axis and liquidity is measured as ease of access (A) along the horizontal axis, assets being most liquid at zero and becoming more illiquid the further we are along the horizontal axis. One measure would be the number of days' notice required before one could liquidate the instrument. As usual, the more illiquid the instrument, the higher the return. If there were no other constraints, one should observe a continuous spectrum of assets from zero-yield, zero-illiquidity (ready cash) to the highest yield on the most illiquid instrument. If we then had consumers with diverse tastes, they could choose their most preferred instruments along such a frontier depending on their marginal rates of substitution between the two characteristics.

Unfortunately, we do not have data on consumer holdings of different financial instruments, even in the aggregate, let alone by individual consumers. What we do observe is the range of products available. In as much as they are available, i.e. being actively offered, we shall assume that they satisfy some consumers'

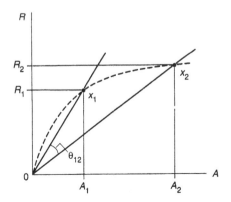

Figure 6.1 Two instruments: x_1 and x_2.

preferences. In the absence of consumer holding data, we have to concentrate on product descriptions to locate the gap.

In Figure 6.1 then, we have two assets available, x_1 and x_2: x_1 offers low yield and high liquidity and x_2 offers high yield and low liquidity. These are points in the characteristics space. We join them to the origin, but we must be careful to avoid thinking that any combination along $0x_1$ (or $0x_2$) is also available. What is offered is the combination x_1 with coordinates $0R_1$ and $0A_1$; similarly for x_2.

The point of joining them to the origin is that now we can define 'nearness' of assets and the gap between assets. Think first of a cosy oligopoly case where every firm offered two instruments, e.g. demand deposits, with implicit return R_1 and ease of access A_1 and time deposits with yield R_2 and ease of access A_2. If all firms offered the same or similar terms, then all the available product points would be closely clustered around x_1 and x_2. There could be $2N$ instruments offered by N firms but in fact these would represent only two instruments. Very close but slightly differentiated products could be offered, e.g. interest rates calculated daily rather than on the balance at the end of the week. But most other differentiation might involve adding unimportant characteristics: multicoloured cheque books, etc.

The distance between the two instruments can then be measured by the angle between them, measured at the origin (cf. equation (8) in Chapter 3). If we knew where the frontier was, we could measure the arc length between the two instruments at the frontier. Thus we take θ_{12}, the angle between x_1 and x_2, as the measure of distance rather than the arc length x_1x_2. (The closer x_1 is to x_2, the less would the two measures diverge.)

We can now illustrate what we mean by trivial and important innovations. In Figure 6.2, x_3 is a very close substitute for x_1 and the distance between them, θ_{13}, is very small. If we only had x_1, x_2 and x_3, the *maximum* distance *after* the introduction of the new asset x_3 between neighbouring assets, $\max(\theta_{13}, \theta_{23})$, would not be very different from the maximum distance *before* its introduction, which was θ_{12}. On the other hand, if x_4 was introduced to a world where only x_1 and x_2 are present, the maximum distance between neighbouring assets would be given by $\max(\theta_{14}, \theta_{24})$ and this distance would be much reduced as a result of the introduction of the new asset. Thus x_4 *fills the gap* in the product range, while x_3 does not.

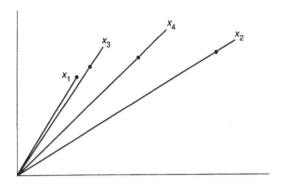

Figure 6.2 A trivial innovation (x_3) and an important innovation (x_4).

Over time the number of assets will change. Let us assume the number of assets will increase. Assume N_t is the total number of instruments at t and N_t will change with t. Now let the maximum distance between adjacent assets at t be θ_t^*, i.e. $\theta_t^* = \max(\theta_{i,i+1;t};$ all $i \in N_t)$. A measure of how innovative a financial market is would be the change in θ_t^* (cf. equation (18) in Chapter 3). Over time one would expect innovations to fill in all the gaps so that the spectrum of assets will be a continuum. This would mean that θ_t^* will decline to zero over time—the gap would vanish. Of course, it is always possible that while assets are getting 'crowded' in the two-characteristics space, there will be a great incentive to innovate by providing a new characteristic (see Section 3.3.3 above). This, of course, is a limiting case. But as long as we can confine ourselves to the two-characteristics space, these two measures are sufficient for our purposes: (1) the distribution of $\theta_{i,i+1}$ at a point of time and (2) the trend in θ_t^* over time.

6.3 Data and measurement

In this section we proceed to measure the distance between assets over time using British monthly data on financial instruments available to British households. In order to collect data that were not only accessible to us but also, in principle, available to ordinary households, we gathered the information from the family finance page of the Saturday edition of *The Times*. This is an easily accessible source. There is obviously some sample selection bias since only the more 'successful' of the instruments would be included.

We found, however, that new instruments were added to the list almost constantly. Where necessary, we filled in additional details on characteristics, etc., from a specialist source, namely the *Investors' Chronicle.*

The financial assets we had information on can be grouped under the principal suppliers: banks, money market funds, National Savings and building societies. For each of these groups, one could proliferate information by using assets which were near substitutes. Thus all the banks provide a similar menu of deposit accounts: 7-day, 30-day, 90-day, 180-day and annual. We noted a specific bank's asset only if it was listed in the source as different. The same goes for building societies. Rather than note each separate society we looked at the types of accounts available: ordinary share, term share, regular saving, etc. On money market funds we found that there was some difference in the yield being offered and so each fund was noted separately.

The data were gathered on a monthly basis as of the last Saturday of each month, from January 1982 to December 1984, giving us 36 time periods. For each month, we took all the financial instruments listed in *The Times* and noted all the characteristics that were given. These were: rate of interest (return), whether gross or net; frequency of interest payment; number of days of notice required; minimum and maximum amounts that could be invested; the term of the instrument; minimum amount for withdrawal; any penalties that would be incurred by premature withdrawal, etc. There are thus clearly a lot of relevant characteristics besides return and access. We will concentrate our analysis on these two key characteristics, however, and largely disregard the others, although we could make the case that many of the other characteristics could be subsumed into one of the two characteristics.[1] Thus by describing yield not as a single number but as a function we could incorporate aspects such as frequency of payment, penalties, term, etc. Similarly, the conditions on amount to be deposited, limits on withdrawal, etc., are elements of the access variable if taken as a function rather than as a scalar. In fact, we conduct a very limited experiment of this below by converting the minimum deposit into days' equivalent of access.

In Table 6.1 we give the information for January 1984 as an illustration. There are more than 30 entries. For all of them we have data

1 See footnote 5 in Chapter 2 and Section 5.3.

Table 6.1 Financial assets available to households in January 1984

Asset		Return to 30% taxpayer	Days' notice	Minimum (£)	Maximum (£)	Term (days/ years)
Banks						
	7D	3.85	7	—	—	
	30D	5.69	30	10 000	25 000	30 d
	90D	5.78	90	10 000	25 000	90 d
	180D	5.95	180	10 000	25 000	180 d
	365D	5.95	365	10 000	25 000	365 d
	Monthly Y	6.39	—	—	—	—
	Lloyds X	6.30	—	—	—	—
Money market funds						
Simco 7D		6.08	7	10 000	—	—
UDT		6.04	7	5000	—	—
Tyndall 7D		6.13	7	2500	—	—
Simco $		—	—	—	—	—
Western Trust		6.06	0	2000	—	—
Millanhall		6.20	0	5000	—	—
Save & Prosper		6.01	0	2500	—	—
Money Market Trust		6.26	7	2500	—	—
Tullet & Riley Call		6.08	0	10 000	—	—
Tullet & Riley 7D		6.16	7	2500	—	—
Schroder 7D		6.04	7	—	—	—
Aitken-Hume		6.06	0	2500	—	—
Britannia		6.21	0	2500	—	—
Schroder-Wagg		—	—	—	—	—
Tyndall Call		6.15	0	2500	—	—
Bank of Scotland		6.22	0	2500	—	—
Charterhouse		6.30	0	2500	—	—
Choularton		—	1	1 000	—	—
M&G Klein		—	0	2500	—	—
Midland HKA		—	—	—	—	—
Henderson		—	0	2500	—	—
HFC		—	7	2500	—	—
National Savings						
Ordinary account		3.6	0	1	10 000	—
Investment account		7.7	31	1	200 000	—
Index-linked bond		4.8	38	10	10 000	5 yr
Certificate		8.26	8	25	5000	5 yr
Income bond		8.05	90	1000	200 000	—
Deposit bond		8.05	90	500	50 000	—
Yearly plan		—	—	20	200/mth	5 yr
Building societies						
Ordinary share		7.25	7	0	30 000	—
Term share		7.75–9.25	90	1000	30 000	1–5 yr
Regular savings		8.50	—	—	—	—
Extra-interest		8.25	—	—	—	—
7D share		—	7	500	30 000	—
28D share		—	28	500	30 000	—
90D share		—	90	500	30 000	—

Table 6.2 Number of assets over time (*N*$_t$)

	1982	1983	1984
January	10	14	23
February	10	14	23
March	10	18	23
April	11	18	23
May	11	20	27
June	11	21	27
July	11	22	28
August	12	22	28
September	12	22	28
October	13	23	28
November	13	23	28
December	13	23	28

on the rate of interest and also whether it was gross or net of taxation. We then have fairly full data on period of notice (access), minimum and maximum deposit and the term of the asset. It is clear from the table that data on these other characteristics can get rather patchy. This slimmed down the number of assets we could analyse.

In Table 6.2 we give therefore the data on the total number of assets used in the analysis. This variable is labelled N_t, the number of assets for month t. We can see that there was a rapid growth in N_t over the three years from 10 in January 1982 to 28 in December 1984. In no month was the number lower than the month before, i.e. $N_{t+1} \geq N_t$ for all t (Figure 6.3). There are big jumps in March 1983 and May 1984, when the number goes from 14 in the previous month to 18 (1983) and 23 to 27 (1984). The growth in March 1983 is explained by the launching of four new money market funds: Money Market Trust, Tullet & Riley Call, Tullet & Riley 7 Day, and Schroder. In May 1984 it was the building societies which launched new types of accounts. This set of innovations meant changing the characteristic of an old asset—the ordinary share account—and launching three new types of shares: 7-day, 28-day and 90-day. The statutory notice (not actually very rigidly applied) before withdrawal from the ordinary share account was formally abolished. The details on all the 28 assets in December 1984 are given in Table 6.3. This shows the date of introduction of the new assets and the assets already existing in January 1982.

Let us look more closely at the data for April 1982. The data are given in Table 6.4 and Figure 6.4 illustrates them. We will examine

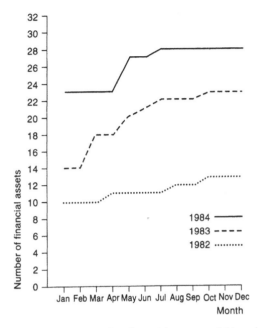

Figure 6.3 The growth in financial assets available to households.

our assets in two-characteristics space. The idea is to see whether we can locate and measure the gap in the asset structure and whether new innovations appear to fill the gap. Figure 6.4 corresponds to Figure 6.2, but now we have actual data. On the vertical axis we have yield net of tax and on the horizontal axis we have days' notice as a measure of access. In order to avoid a bunching of many assets at 0 days or 7 days we also took into account the minimum amount that could be accepted as a deposit. We saw the minimum amount as an additional illiquidity characteristic and added (admittedly arbitrarily) one day for each £100. Thus a 7-day account with £1000 minimum was taken to be 17 days. As we see from Table 6.2, the first new asset arrives in April 1982 and we also know which one it is: Western Trust (G in Figure 6.4), a new money market fund with a yield of 9.14%, no notice but a minimum deposit of £2000. The various assets appear as points in the two-characteristics space. At the left, we have the building society ordinary share account which had a yield of 8.75% and 7-day notice and no minimum. Next to it is the National Savings Certificate with a yield of 8.92%,

Table 6.3 Assets and their dates of introduction

Asset	Date of introduction or change[a]
Banks	
7D	
30D	
Money market funds	
Simco	(October 1983)
UDT	
Tyndall 7D	
Western Trust	April 1982
Millanhall	August 1982 (April 1984)
Save & Prosper	January 1983
Money Market Trust	March 1983
Tullet & Riley Call	March 1983
Tullet & Riley 7D	March 1983
Schroder	March 1983
Aitken-Hume	May 1983
Britannia	May 1983
Tyndall Call	July 1983
Bank of Scotland	June 1983
Henderson	May 1984
HFC	July 1984
National Savings	
Ordinary account	
Investment account	
Index-linked bond	
Certificate	
Income bond	October 1982 (April 1983)
Deposit bond	October 1983
Building societies	
Ordinary share	(May 1984)
7D share	May 1984
28D share	May 1984
90D share	May 1984

Note

a No date given implies the asset existed in January 1982. Dates in parentheses signify major changes in characteristics other than yield. Number of assets: January 1982 = 10; December 1984 = 28.

8-day notice and a minimum of £25. There is alongside, but below it, the 7-day bank account which only gives 7.18%.

Now rational economic theory would predict that this asset should not be offered at all as it is dominated by other assets, i.e. it is in the interior rather than on the frontier. Other assets, such as

Building Society Term Share 1, are in a similar situation. How is it possible for such inefficient assets to exist? Our answer is that there are additional characteristics not specified here which account for this anomaly. These assets are available and popular enough to be listed in *The Times*. They presumably meet consumer demand and have characteristics which explain their continued existence. This argument is not necessarily circular. These assets continue to exist over the entire 36-month period. We cannot merely invoke consumer irrationality or habit persistence to account for their presence.

Using Figure 6.4 we can also remark on how the assets spread. At the high access end up to 7–8 days' notice we have building societies, banks and National Savings, all requiring no minimum or a negligible minimum. Next there are money market funds which offer a higher yield for the same notice but require a minimum. These are Simco 7-day (S7), offering 8.64%, 7-day and £1000 minimum, and Tyndall 7-day (T7), offering 8.75%, 7-day and £2500 minimum. Between these two we have the National Savings Investment Account which offers a higher interest rate of 9.45%, no minimum but 30 days' notice. Western Trust then exploits the gap between S7 and the National Savings Investment Account by offering 9.14% for no notice, but a £2000 minimum. We observe Western Trust coming between S7 and T7, both money market funds. Its proximity to the National Savings Investment Account may be real, i.e. a conscious effort to compete, or it may be a trivial addition since different types of households buy money market funds as against NS certificates.

Further to the right on the illiquid side, the banks' 30-day account with a yield of 8.75% and £10 000 minimum defines one extreme. (The 90-day account with £10 000 minimum is not drawn here. It offers a yield lower than the banks' 30-day account which appears to be anomalous.) Building societies offer term shares at either 9.75% or 10.75%, with 90 days' notice and a £500 minimum. These must surely dominate banks' 90-day accounts. In the gap between the 7-day and the 30-day/90-day assets, the money market fund UDT appears. By offering 9.37% for 7 days' notice with a minimum of £5000, it caters for the large saver who does not wish to stay illiquid for any great length of time.

The money market funds as a group, S7, WT, T7 and UDT, thus fill a gap between the short-term and long-term accounts offered by the banks and the building societies. National Savings competes

Table 6.4 Financial assets available to households in April 1982

Key[a]	Asset	Return to 30% taxpayer	Days' notice	Minimum (£)	Maximum (£)	Term (days/years)
Banks						
A	7D	7.18	7	—	—	—
B	30D	8.75	30	10 000	—	30 d
C	90D	8.40	90	10 000	—	90 d
	180D	—	180	10 000	—	180 d
	365D	—	365	10 000	—	365 d
	Monthly Y	—	—	—	—	—
	Lloyds X	—	—	—	—	—
Money market funds						
D	Simco 7D	8.64	7	1000	—	—
E	UDT	9.37	7	5000	—	—
F	Tyndall 7D	8.75	7	2500	—	—
	Simco §	9.74	—	—	—	—
G	Western Trust	9.14	0	2000	—	—
	Millanhall	—	—	—	—	—
	Save & Prosper	—	—	—	—	—
	Money Market Trust	—	—	—	—	—
	Tullet & Riley Call	—	—	—	—	—
	Tullet & Riley 7D	—	—	—	—	—
	Schroder 7D	—	—	—	—	—
	Aitken-Hume	—	—	—	—	—
	Britannia	—	—	—	—	—

Schroder-Wagg	—	—	—	—	—
Tyndall Call	—	—	—	—	—
Bank of Scotland	—	—	—	—	—
Charterhouse	—	—	—	—	—
Choularton	—	—	—	—	—
M&G Klein	—	—	—	—	—
Midland HK A	—	—	—	—	—
Henderson	—	—	—	—	—
HFC	—	—	—	—	—
National Savings					
H Ordinary account	5.0	0	—	—	—
I Investment account	9.45	30	1	200 000	—
Index-linked bond	—	8	10	5000	5yr
J Certificate	8.92	8	25	5000	5yr
Income bond	—	—	—	—	—
Deposit bond	—	—	—	—	—
Yearly plan	—	—	—	—	—
Building societies					
K Ordinary share	8.75	7	0	30 000	—
L Term share	9.25–10.75	90	500	30 000	1–5yr
Regular savings	10.0	—	—	—	—
Extra-interest	—	—	—	—	—
7D share	—	—	—	—	—
28D share	—	—	—	—	—
90D share	—	—	—	—	—

Note
a See Figure 6.4.

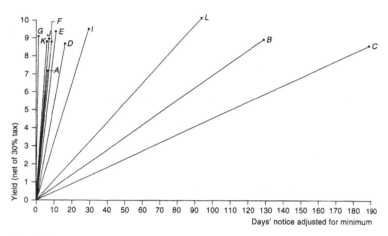

Figure 6.4 Financial assets available to households in April 1982.

with 7-day accounts and presumably with money market funds. From Figure 6.4, however, we can see that there are still gaps for new assets to fill. Western Trust appeared in April 1982 in the gap between S7 and T7, but there are further gaps between T7 and UDT or UDT and Building Society Term 2, etc.

We could draw the analogue of Figure 6.4 for each month but that would give too much detail. We present two more figures, one for May 1983, where the total number of assets is 20 (Figure 6.5 and Table 6.5), and one for May 1984, where the total is 27 (Figure 6.6 and Table 6.6). The definitions of the axes are the same as before and the assets which continue on from the old date are labelled in the same way.

We notice immediately that Figures 6.5 and 6.6 are much more 'crowded' than Figure 6.4. In Figure 6.5, there are many more assets in the middle range previously occupied by the money market funds apart from the National Savings Investment Account. Between S7 and UDT Account, there were three assets in April 1982: WT, T7 and the National Savings Investment Account; now there are ten assets in that gap. The rate of introduction of new assets is slow at first: one in August 1982 (Millanhall MM Fund), one in October 1982 (National Savings Income Bond), one in January 1983 (Save & Prosper MM Fund). Then there is an explosion in March 1983 with four new money market funds (Tullet & Riley Call and 7-Day, Schroder and Money Market Trust). This is followed by two

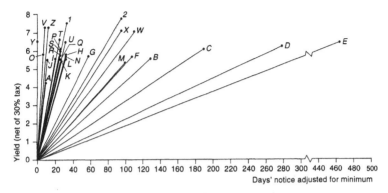

Figure 6.5 Financial assets available to households in May 1983.

more in May 1983 (Aitken-Hume and Britannia). Except for the National Savings Income Bond, all the others are money market funds filling in the small gaps in the S7–UDT range. The left-hand side of the figure covering short-term accounts is relatively undisturbed. Generally yields are lower in May 1983 than in April 1982 but the spread is similar. At the long end, National Savings Income bond (NSY) and Tullet & Riley Call with £10 000 minimum seem to fill in the gap between Building Society Term 1 and Term 2.

We see then that between April 1982 and May 1983 the major innovations come from 'follower' money market funds which observe the gap left by the leaders S7, T7, WT, UDT. Only the Tullet & Riley Call fund with £10 000 minimum is analogous to a Building Society Term Account. It is here that the National Savings Income Bond offering 7.7%, 90-day and £2000 minimum comes in to compete with the building societies' 6.75–7.25%, 90-day, £500 minimum term shares.

It is the gap at the long end that gets filled by May 1984. Between May 1983 and May 1984, there is again a slow growth to begin with. Money market funds continue to appear: one in June 1983 (Bank of Scotland), one in July 1983 (Tyndall Call). But after that there is no further action in money market funds until May 1984, when Henderson appears. The big explosion is at the long end. National Savings improved their income bond in April 1983 and launched the deposit bond in October 1983. But it was the building societies which fought back by improving the yield and conditions on their term shares. They introduced 7-day, 28-day and 90-day

Table 6.5 Financial assets available to households in May 1983

Key[a]	Asset	Return to 30% taxpayer	Days' notice	Minimum (£)	Maximum (£)	Term (days/years)
Banks						
A	7D	4.73	7	—		—
B	30D	6.48	30	10 000	25 000	30 d
C	90D	6.30	90	10 000	25 000	90 d
D	180D	6.21	180	10 000	25 000	180 d
E	365D	6.21	365	10 000	25 000	365 d
	Monthly Y	—	—	—	—	—
	Lloyds X	—	—	—	—	—
Money market funds						
F	Simco 7D	6.88	7	1000	—	—
G	UDT	6.83	7	5000	—	—
H	Tyndall 7D	7.00	7	2500	—	—
	Simco $	5.38	—	—	—	—
	Western Trust	6.87	—	—	—	—
I	Millanhall	6.97	0	5000	—	—
J	Save & Prosper	6.78	0	2500	—	—
K	Money Market Trust	7.01	7	2500	—	—
L	Tullet & Riley Call	7.14	0	10 000	—	—
M	Tullet & Riley 7D	7.08	7	2500	—	—
N	Schroder 7D	6.85	7	—	—	—
O	Aitken-Hume	7.18	0	2500	—	—

		Rate		Min	Max	Term
P	Britannia	7.52	0	2500	—	—
	Schroder-Wagg	—	—	—	—	—
Q	Tyndall Call	6.96	0	2500	—	—
	Bank of Scotland	—	—	—	—	—
	Charterhouse	—	1	2500	—	—
	Choularton	—	—	1000	—	—
	M&G Klein	—	—	—	—	—
	Midland HKA	—	—	—	—	—
	Henderson	—	—	—	—	—
	HFC	—	7	—	—	—
	National Savings					
R	Ordinary account	3.6	0	1	10 000	—
	Investment account	7.35	31	1	200 000	—
S	Index-linked bond	4.60	8	10	10 000	5yr
T	Certificate	7.51	8	25	5 000	5yr
U	Income bond	7.70	90	2000	200 000	—
	Deposit bond	—	90	500	50 000	—
	Yearly plan	—	—	20	200/mth	5yr
	Building societies					
V	Ordinary share	6.25	7	0	30 000	—
W	Term share	6.75–7.25	90	500	30 000	1–5yr
	Regular savings	7.50	—	—	—	—
	Extra-interest	—	—	—	—	—
	7D share	—	7	500	30 000	—
	28D share	—	28	500	30 000	—
	90D share	—	90	500	30 000	—

Note
a See Figure 6.5.

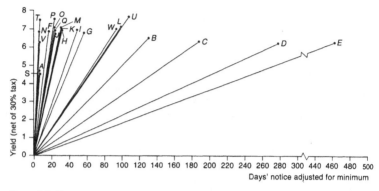

Figure 6.6 Financial assets available to households in May 1984.

shares and formally abolished the 7-day notice on their ordinary share account. The minimum on their term shares was still £500 but the reduction in notice and the spread of 7-day, 28-day and 90-day were the real innovations.

These innovations get the building societies competing across the spectrum. Thus the 28-day competes with money market funds (shown in Figure 6.5 as 1), and the 90-day competes at the long end with National Savings Deposit (NSD) and Income (NSY) Accounts as well as with the high-minimum, low-notice money market funds.

This last bunch of innovations by the building societies is thus retaliatory. They ape the existing assets—money market funds, NS bonds—to restore their market shares. If we had data on market shares, we could make this retaliatory nature of the innovations more precise, but even at the descriptive level, our figures make the point obvious.

The course of financial innovations in Britain over the three years 1982–84 is thus clear. There is a growth in the total class of assets available to the retail depositor from 10 to 28. This growth is monotonic but not smooth. There are periods of slow growth interrupted by sudden bursts but no decline in the number of asset classes. It would seem that initially banks and building societies provided similar products at the short and the long end. Competition came first from National Savings and then more seriously from the money market funds. The money market funds moved into the gap between the 7-day and 30-day assets by offering more attractive—higher yield—assets at the 7-day end. The pro-liferation of assets in this middle range came from 'follower' funds moving in where 'leader' funds had left the gap. The gap was certainly filled by May 1983. The next bunch of innovations came from the building societies. They were responding to National Savings' attempt to cut into their long-end accounts by introducing Income and Deposit Bonds. Their response took the form of offer-ing a wider spread of assets. This put them in a competitive position in the short, middle and long ends. The only non-innovative agents in all this appeared to be the banks. Their hold on the current cheque-book account was threatened only during 1985 when building societies again introduced cheque-save accounts as well as offering electronic cash withdrawals. That, however, takes us outside our sample period.

6.4 An analytical view of innovation

In the previous section, we took a descriptive approach to our data. We listed assets by date, isolated new entrants and projected them on a two-characteristics space. The figures for the three time periods, April 1982, May 1983 and May 1984, seemed to tally with our expectation that gaps will be filled by innovation. But we can go further than that. We can use our θ measures to give slightly greater precision to our understanding of the process.

Recall our definition of θ above. At any point of time t, we measure $\theta_{i,i+1}$ (call it $\hat{\theta}_i$) as the angle between the neighbouring assets. The notion of a neighbouring asset raises no problem in two dimensions. We can look upon the distribution of $\hat{\theta}_i$ for each time period as a measure of the thinness of the market. In a deep market, with many assets closely competing with each other, the $\hat{\theta}_i$ will all be small. If there are gaps, some $\hat{\theta}_i$ will be large, others small.

In Table 6.7, we present the size distribution of $\hat{\theta}_i$ for each month for the entire period. We have divided the full length into 12 size classes. The typical interval is 0.05, starting from 0.00 and ending at 0.55, but over time the maximum length narrows. In some cases, while keeping to 12 size classes, we have narrowed the inter-val to 0.04, ranging from 0.00 to 0.44 (indicated by 'a' in the table) and also to 0.02, ranging from 0.00 to 0.22 (indicated by 'b' in the table).

The table should be seen as a series of histograms, one for each month, but expressed numerically rather than graphically. To begin

Table 6.6 Financial assets available to households in May 1984

Key[a]	Asset	Return to 30% taxpayer	Days' notice	Minimum (£)	Maximum (£)	Term (days/years)
Banks						
A	7D	4.20	7	—	—	—
B	30D	5.51	30	10 000	25 000	30 d
C	90D	6.13	90	10 000	25 000	90 d
D	180D	6.21	180	10 000	25 000	180 d
E	365D	6.48	365	10 000	25 000	365 d
	Monthly Y	6.39	—	—	—	—
	Lloyds X	5.78	—	—	—	—
Money market funds						
F	Simco 7D	5.66	7	10 000	—	—
G	UDT	5.69	7	5000	—	—
H	Tyndall 7D	5.78	7	2500	—	—
	Simco $	—	—	—	—	—
I	Western Trust	5.56	0	2000	—	—
J	Millanhall	5.43	1	1000	—	—
K	Save & Prosper	5.53	0	2500	—	—
L	Money Market Trust	5.74	7	2500	—	—
M	Tullet & Riley Call	5.33	0	10 000	—	—
N	Tullet & Riley 7D	5.74	7	2500	—	—
O	Schroder 7D	5.81	7	—	—	—
P	Aitken-Hume	6.13	0	2500	—	—

Q	Britannia	5.60	0	2 500	—	—
	Schroder-Wagg	—	1	2 500	—	—
R	Tyndall Call	5.74	0	2 500	—	—
S	Bank of Scotland	6.06	0	2 500	—	—
	Charterhouse	—	0	2 500	—	—
	Choularton	—	1	1 000	—	—
	M&G Klein	—	0	2 500	—	—
	Midland HKA	—	—	—	—	—
T	Henderson	6.65	0	2 500	—	—
	HFC	—	7	2 500	—	—
National Savings						
	Ordinary account	3.6	0	1	10 000	—
U	Investment account	6.48	31	1	200 000	—
	Index-linked bond	—	8	10	10 000	5yr
V	Certificate	+7.25	8	25	5000	5yr
W	Income bond	7.00	90	2 000	50 000	—
X	Deposit bond	7.00	90	500	50 000	—
	Yearly plan	—	—	20	200/mth	5yr
Building societies						
Y	Ordinary share	6.25	0	0	30 000	—
	Term share	—	90	1 000	30 000	1–5yr
	Regular savings	7.5	—	—	—	—
	Extra-interest	7.25	—	—	—	—
Z	7D share	7.25	7	500	30 000	—
1	28D share	7.5	28	500	30 000	—
2	90D share	7.75	90	500	30 000	—

Note
a See Figure 6.6.

Table 6.7 Size distribution of $\hat{\theta}_i$ (January 1982 to December 1984)

$\hat{\theta}_i$	1.82	2.82	3.82	4.82	5.82	6.82	7.82	8.82	9.82	10.82	11.82	12.82[a]
0.00(1)	1	1	1	1	3	1	1	3	2	5	7	4
0.05(2)	3	3	5	6	3	5	4	4	6	5	2	5
0.10(3)	4	4		1	2	2	3	2	1	1	1	1
0.15(4)			2	2	2	2	1	1	1			1
0.20(5)										1	1	
0.25(6)	1	1	1				1	1			1	1
0.30(7)									1			
0.35(8)							1	1	1			1
0.40(9)											1	
0.45(10)			1									
0.50(11)		1		1	1	1				1		
0.55(12)	1											

$\hat{\theta}_i$	1.83	2.83	3.83	4.83[a]	5.83[a]	6.83[a]	7.83	8.83[b]	9.83[b]	10.83[a]	11.83	12.83
0.00(1)	5	6	8	6	9	14	14	10	11	16	16	16
0.05(2)	5	3	4	6	7	3	4	4	3	4	4	4
0.10(3)	2	3	2	2	2	2		4	3	1		
0.15(4)	2		1					1	1	3		
0.20(5)												
0.25(6)				1	1	1	1				1	1
0.30(7)			1				1			1		
0.35(8)	1	1		1	1	1						
0.40(9)												
0.45(10)											1	1
0.50(11)										1	1	
0.55(12)								1				

$\hat{\theta}_i$	1.84[a]	2.84[a]	3.84[a]	4.84[b]	5.84[b]	6.84[b]	7.84	8.84	9.84[a]	10.84[a]	11.84[a]	12.84[a]
0.00(1)	17	17	18	12	11	12	17	18	18	18	18	18
0.05(2)	3	3	2	6	5	5	5	5	3	3	4	4
0.10(3)		1	1	2	3	2	1	1	2	2	2	2
0.15(4)							1	1		1	1	
0.20(5)				1	1	1						
0.25(6)					1							
0.30(7)	1	1						1	1	1		
0.35(8)			1							1	1	1
0.40(9)												
0.45(10)												
0.50(11)												
0.55(12)				1		1	1					

Notes
a Interval 0.04, range 0.00–0.44.
b Interval 0.02, range 0.00–0.22.
1.82 means January 1982, etc.

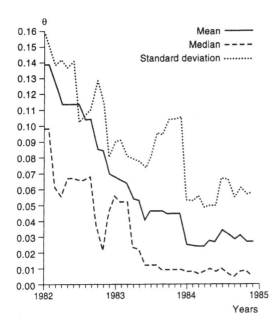

Figure 6.7 The change in θ over time.

with, we see in January 1982 that the mode occurs at 0.10, the bulk of the distribution is below that (8 out 10) but there are some extreme values, e.g. 0.55. There are two gaps. Over time, the distances diminish on average, i.e. the mean value of $\hat{\theta}_i$ for each t goes down over time. This is presented in Figure 6.7. We can see that there is a mild but definite downward trend in the mean of $\hat{\theta}_i$: it falls from 0.139 to 0.027. The movement is not monotonic, i.e. the curve is bumpy and there is a rise in the value sometimes. This may be due to macroeconomic factors such as changes in nominal interest rates 'opening out' some gaps when they rise and eliminating them when rates fall. Over time, however, the average $\hat{\theta}_i$ falls.

Further, the distribution is squashed nearer to the zero value, i.e. there are an increasing number of closely competing assets. The first size class (0.00) has the largest number, i.e. becomes the mode most emphatically by February 1983 and stays the modal value. The first size class is also the median consistently after June 1983. (There are earlier instances when 0.00 is the mode or the median but we ignore these.) Thus the median follows the mean, falling from 0.098 in January 1982 to 0.005 in December 1984.

There is thus a decline in the mean over time, and the mode as well since the median occurs in the first size class quite early on. This is a sure indicator of assets increasingly being seen as close substitutes for each other. There is also evidence of increasing homogeneity, i.e. an increasing degree of the market, since the standard deviation of $\hat{\theta}_i$ also shows a downward trend. As Table 6.7 indicates, the standard deviation goes from 0.160 in January 1982 to 0.058 in December 1984. Again, while there are fluctuations in this figure, the trend is definitely downwards.

Thus we have found evidence of the increasing presence of assets that are close substitutes. We still need to look further, however. Recall that in the discussion of the theoretical framework above we made a distinction between trivial and important innovations. An explosion in trivial innovations will reduce $\hat{\theta}_i$ over time in mean, median and mode. This could happen while the gaps stay wide open. We need therefore an additional measure. This is the measure of θ_t^*, the maximum of the $\hat{\theta}_i$. If there are important innovations, θ_t^* should go down over time as well.

The time path of the maximum angle θ_t^* can be seen in Table 6.8. To begin with we have $\hat{\theta}_i$ as large as 0.55 in January 1982. This corresponds to the highest range in which an observation occurs in Table 6.7. As the highest range in which an observation occurs moves down, we see that θ_t^* falls correspondingly. The time path of θ_t^* is not, however, monotonically downwards. It goes up and down. Over the period as a whole, it goes down from 0.55 in January 1982 to 0.28 in December 1984. The lowest it gets is 0.22 in mid-1984. There is thus a closing of the gap over time and although there are 'copycat' new products, as we saw above for May 1983, there are sufficient new distinctive products to lower the maximum gap (see also Figure 6.8).

Although the largest gap is on a downward trend over time, our data enable us to ask one further question. Do new products always appear where the gap is the largest? Do we, in other words, see potential producers of new products as scanning the market, finding the largest gap and then tailoring their new product to fit the gap? If this were so, it would mean that our method of locating the gap simultaneously locates the most profitable opportunity for a new entrant. This is, of course, not necessarily so. Higher profits may be made by locating closer to existing products than locating in a large gap. This is what happens in April 1982. As of March 1982, the distribution of $\hat{\theta}_i$ shows a clustering of six out of ten assets into the

Table 6.8 θ_t^*: the maximum gap

Date	θ_t^*
January 1982	0.55
February 1982	0.50
March 1982	0.45
April 1982	0.50
May 1982	0.50
June 1982	0.50
July 1982	0.35
August 1982	0.35
September 1982	0.35
October 1982	0.50
November 1982	0.40
December 1982	0.28
January 1983	0.40
February 1983	0.40
March 1983	0.30
April 1983	0.28
May 1983	0.28
June 1983	0.28
July 1983	0.30
August 1983	0.22
September 1983	0.20
October 1983	0.24
November 1983	0.45
December 1983	0.45
January 1984	0.24
February 1984	0.24
March 1984	0.28
April 1984	0.22
May 1984	0.22
June 1984	0.22
July 1984	0.22
August 1984	0.30
September 1984	0.24
October 1984	0.28
November 1984	0.28
December 1984	0.28

first two intervals (0.00 and 0.05). This was followed by a gap of one interval and two more assets were in the fourth interval (0.15), again followed by one gap to one more asset at 0.25. The maximum gap was between 0.25 and 0.55, where the last asset appeared. In April 1982, the new asset appeared not in the gap between 0.25 and 0.55, but between 0.05 and 0.15. We saw this in Figure 6.3. The

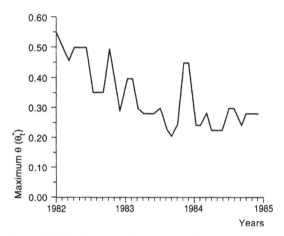

Figure 6.8 The change in the maximum θ over time.

biggest gap is between UDT and the Building Society Term Shares. Leaving the National Savings Investment Account out of consideration for the time being, it would seem that the gap between S7 and T7 is the second largest one, and this is where the new product WT appears. Thus from the potential entrant's point of view, we have to translate the size of the *ex ante* gaps into *ex ante* profitability. This requires data on market shares of existing assets which were not available to us. It is interesting to note, however, that the new product appears in the second largest if not the largest gap.

To translate the gap into *ex ante* profitability we need some further information on the volume transacted in these assets. Thus think of a producer of financial assets thinking *ex ante* of entering the market. He locates various gaps. Corresponding to a large gap $\hat{\theta}_i$ there will be two 'neighbouring' assets x_i and x_{i+1} with which he will compete. His expected profits will depend upon the volumes transacted in x_i and x_{i+1} and the share of these volumes that the potential entrant can entice away from these two neighbouring assets, minus the cost of the interest/access combination he offers to his depositors. This could be formally set out very easily. (See Deshmukh *et al.* (1983) for a similar problem and its formulation.)

A very interesting implication of the pattern of innovations as revealed by Figures 6.4–6.6 and the statistics in Table 6.7 should be

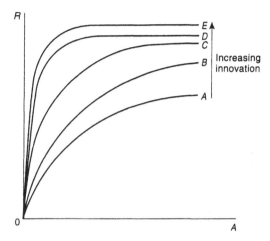

Figure 6.9 The limit to financial innovation.

pointed out. Ideally the frontier between R and A should be concave, as is drawn in Figure 6.1, i.e. higher illiquidity has to be suffered if higher return is required. A consequence of innovations has been to make instruments more and more liquid without sacrificing return. This is a consequence of the rapid development in electronic technology which allows suppliers of these instruments to maintain minimal cash reserves against probable withdrawal. By insisting on a very short period of notice before withdrawal, say one day or even less, and by discouraging multiple withdrawals of small amounts, financial firms can guard against having to maintain costly inventories of cash at clearing banks. This enables more and more highly liquid instruments to be supplied profitably. In terms of the diagram in Figure 6.1, the frontier shifts upwards and to the left. The trade-off between return and liquidity gets higher and higher $(\delta(dR/dA)/\delta t > 0)$. One can therefore imagine that in the limit the frontier could become '⌈' shaped, steep at the short liquid end and flat in the large range of illiquidity (as shown by line E in Figure 6.9).

If such a process occurs, the effect is to render the financial market highly liquid and hence subject to volatile changes in the volume of transactions as depositors quickly and, nearly costlessly, move funds from one asset to another. In this sense, the volatility of the financial system could increase as innovations occur.

6.5   Conclusion

We would claim that the measures $\hat{\theta}_i$ and θ_t^* are useful and interesting indicators of the process of innovation. They tell us about the state of the market at a point in time, as well as its evolution over the course of time. The attempt to define gaps in characteristics space in terms of angles seems to give an intuitively plausible way of looking at the problem.

There are several directions for future research. First, we should try to extend our data set by getting information on individual banks and building societies as well as money market funds. It would also be most helpful if we could obtain information on the amount invested in these different assets and hence on market shares.

We also need to look at the multiple-characteristic case. However, this is not at all straightforward as we move from two to many characteristics since the notions of 'nearness' and of 'gap' are not easily amenable to intuitive interpretation in many dimensions (see Lancaster (1982) for a discussion).

References

Bank of England (1983). The nature and implications of financial innovations. *Quarterly Bulletin*, September, 358–76.

Deshmukh, S. D., Greenbaum, S. I. and Kanatas, G. (1983). Interest rate uncertainty and the financial intermediary's choice of exposure. *Journal of Finance*, 38, 141–47.

Federal Reserve Board of New York (1981–82). Innovations in the financial markets. *Quarterly Review*, Winter, 1–41.

Greenbaum, S. I. and Heywood, C. V. (1973). Secular change in the financial services industry. *Journal of Money, Credit and Banking*, 3, 571–89.

Lancaster, K. (1982). Innovative entry: Profit hidden beneath the zero. *Journal of Industrial Economics*, 31, 41–56.

Rosen, S. (1974). Hedonic process and implicit markets: Product differentiation in pure competition. *Journal of Political Economy*, 82, 34–55.

Silber, W. L. (1975). Towards a theory of financial innovation. In *Financial Innovations*. Lexington, Mass.: D.C. Heath.

Silber, W. L. (1983). The process of financial innovation. *American Economic Review*, 73, 89–95.

Chapter 7

Postscript

David Blake

We hope we have shown that the characteristics model provides an ideal framework for analysing both theoretically and empirically all aspects of the financial system, from portfolio behaviour and asset pricing, through financial intermediation and financial innovation, to the regulatory structure of the financial system itself.

We believe that the particular usefulness of the characteristics model lies in its empirical applications. The financial system generates masses of high-quality data on the characteristics of financial assets, economic agents and financial institutions.

However, these data are expensive to collect and process and are also often regarded as confidential by those organisations that collect them. It is therefore often difficult for researchers to gain access to them. Furthermore, since the data have not generally been collected expressly for the purpose of academic research, they are often not complete or in a form readily usable by researchers.

In addition, there can be a proliferation of measured characteristics, yet the real benefit of the characteristics model comes from being able to explain the behaviour of a large number of variables in terms of a much smaller set of common characteristics. To preserve the model's usefulness as an empirical tool, it is necessary to continue to work with a small number of key characteristics and to convert the remaining minor characteristics into 'equivalences' of the key characteristics which are then aggregated with these key characteristics.

Attempts were made to do this in the empirical chapters above, e.g. the computation of interest equivalences in Chapter 5 and the conversion of the minimum deposit size into days' equivalent of access in Chapter 6. However, we recognised that these conversions were often very arbitrary. Much more thorough experimentation needs to take place before we can be confident that we have found satisfactory characteristics models that explain different features of the financial system in terms of a small number of characteristics and their equivalences.

Furthermore, the empirical models analysed above were confined to the personal financial services sector. But as new and more comprehensive data sets become available, other sectors of the financial system become amenable to empirical analysis, including the wholesale sector, the corporate sector, financial intermediaries, and the international sector.

It is immediately apparent where future research in this field must be directed: new data sets on financial characteristics must be accessed and analysed, and greater experimentation in the conversion of minor characteristics into equivalences of the major characteristics needs to be conducted. Only when this research agenda has been completed will the richness of the financial applications of the characteristics model be fully appreciated.

Index

Absolute risk tolerance, 28, 29
α–τ model, 22
Arbitrage-free models, 19
ARCH-in-mean pricing model, 30
Arrow–Debreu price, 21
Asset-characteristics space, 7, 8
Asset-characteristics technology, 3,
   14–16, 21, 23, 26, 41, 42, 49
Asset pricing, 3, 12, 19, 127
Asset transformation, 37, 38
Assets, 14
Autoregressive conditional
   heteroscedasticity, 31

Banking industry, 84
Banks, 7, 104
Basis risk, 38
Bellman's principle of optimality, 27
Below mean semi-variance
   preference model, 22
Big Bang, 70–73
Bonds, 61
Building societies, 7, 84, 104

Capital asset pricing model, 23
Characteristics, 1, 13–16, 21, 23, 26,
   29, 35, 39–42, 51, 57, 58, 87, 101,
   104
Characteristics model, 1, 2, 12, 13,
   14, 21, 23, 26, 28, 30, 35, 36, 39,
   56–58, 76, 78, 97, 127
Conditional variance, 31
Constraint-induced innovations, 47
Convenience of location, 2

Cost function, 14–15
Crash of 1987, 5, 70
Current accounts, 5, 60

Default risk, 38
Degree of financial innovation, 50
Degree of financial intermediation,
   42–43, 44
Demand for related goods, 1
Deposit-taking institution, 49
Deposits, 60, 61, 63
Derived demand, 15–16
Diversification, 38
Divisibility, 13, 39

Efficiency frontier, 5, 6, 14, 26, 59, 69
Efficiency plane, 60, 61
Exchange rate risk, 38
Expected return, 2, 4, 39, 57, 64
Expected utility model, 20
External characteristics, 36, 39, 45

Financial innovation, 4, 8, 17,
   35–37, 44–50, 96, 116, 127
Financial institution, 6, 37, 39, 60,
   97
Financial instrument, 6, 97, 99
Financial intermediary, 4, 37, 41,
   43, 48, 100
Financial intermediation, 4, 35, 36,
   37–44, 127
Financial market, 56, 57, 78, 97,
   103
Financial options, 50

Financial product, 2, 4, 7, 37, 57–63, 78, 83, 99
Financial products box, 61

Generalised ARCH, 31

Higher-interest chequing account, 84, 86, 87, 88
Higher-interest deposit account, 84, 87, 88

Illiquidity, 59, 66, 101, 125
Implicit interest, 85
Inflation risk, 38, 96
Innovation strategy, 48
Insurance, 37, 62
Interest, 2
Interest equivalence, 6, 89, 92
Interest rate risk, 38
Intermediate claims, 37
Internal characteristics, 36, 39–41, 49
Intertemporal capital asset pricing model, 26
Investment bank, 43

Linear pricing rules, 19
Liquidity, 2–4, 13, 37, 39, 57, 58, 60, 62, 64, 77, 101, 125
Liquidity risk, 38
Loans, 60
Location, 39, 76, 101
London Stock Exchange, 5, 70

Market makers, 73
Market portfolio, 19, 28
Marketability, 2
Maturity, 39
Maturity transformation, 37
Maximum withdrawal, 89
Mean function, 21
Mean-risk preference model, 21
Mean-variance preference model, 22
Minimum cheque constraint, 88
Minimum deposit requirement, 88
Minimum investment requirement, 88
Money, 61, 63, 78

Money market funds, 7, 104
Money transmission, 37
Mortgages, 84
Multi-beta model, 29
National Savings, 7, 60, 104
Nonprice characteristics, 6, 83, 84, 85, 88, 89, 92

Parameter-preference model, 21
Payoff function, 20–21
Personal loans, 84, 87, 89, 94
Policy reaction function, 48, 79
Portfolio behaviour, 3, 12, 127
Portfolio decisions, 20
Portfolio management products, 62
Predictability of value, 13
Price risk, 38
Primary borrower, 37, 39, 41
Primary claims, 37
Primary liabilities, 41
Processing of information, 37
Property, 60
Prospective yield, 13

Regulation-induced innovations, 47
Regulations, 36, 47, 51, 63
Regulatory authority, 48
Repayment mortgages, 84, 87, 89, 94
Retail banking, 84, 88
Return, 57, 101, 104, 125
Reversibility, 13, 25, 39
Risk, 2, 3, 30, 32, 39, 57, 60, 62, 78
Risk function, 21
Risk transformation, 38
Riskless asset, 19, 28

SEAQ, 71, 73
SEAQ Automated Execution Facility, 71, 73
Securitisation, 51
Security, 2, 4, 57, 59
Shadow price, 21, 40, 48, 51
Single-beta model, 29
State-contingent prices, 20
State-preference model, 20
Stochastic investment opportunities, 26

Target semi-variance preference
  model, 22
Technical progress, 67–69, 78
Technological change, 63, 77, 97
Technology, 36, 47, 51
Technology-induced innovations, 47
Transactions costs, 37, 77
Transformation of maturities, 37

Ultimate assets, 41, 42
Ultimate claims, 37
Ultimate lender, 37, 39, 40
Utility function, 15, 20, 27, 40

Yield, 13, 77, 101

Printed in the United States
by Baker & Taylor Publisher Services